I0540382

Random Thoughts & F*cked Up Answers

Monique Arge

Inner Workings of...

An Impassioned Mind!

COPYRIGHT... AM I Right?!

All jokes aside, this is my intellectual property.

Who is 'my' you ask?

My is *me*—Monique Arge—the chaotic mind, and proud creator behind these ramblings.

You can find this damaged-goods shot calla' on Instagram, X, TikTok or Facebook on:

@BoldChaosTheory
www.BoldChaosTheory.com

Raw. Uncut.
Cut-up, Me.

This beautifully broken life has *gifted* me with a kaleidoscope of intensely surreal experiences, each one more bizarre and profound than the last.

During the darkest hours of my world when I stretched myself translucent, there was no life lesson that could have prepared me for the pulverizing betrayals that struck me like a spinning backfist through thy soul, as it shattered my dignity and marooned me onto rock-bottom's basement floor.

When I fell to my lowest—stripped to my barest core—life demanded me to get acquainted with the long-overdue shadows of my past: the menacing skeletons in the closet, begging to be dusted off and given their proper eulogy. One filled with love, grace, and a final farewell.

These raw aches and vivid memories softly whispered the varnished reality of my stolen childhood, throwing me on a merciless road while I tried to navigate this world.

Living this life trapped within a mental prison, I heaved the weight of unresolved trauma, born from years of physical and verbal abuse at the hands of my father.

The Old Man's unrelenting pain exacted internal scars upon me as it metastasized into self-ordained cruelty. A legacy I carried from the time I was barely three years old, too young to understand the tempestuous nature to which I was subjected.

It wasn't until my father passed away on January 25, 2020, when an unexpected sense of liberation washed over me. In the rubble of my despair, something extraordinary was unveiled.

A lifesaving, come-to-Jesus wake-up call, jolted me on a path of self-discovery and healing. The red-flagged grains of sand dwindled in my trauma-filled hourglass of a wrecked life.

The final hour for a 180-degree overhaul,

to reboot my core with a rebirth rhapsody, revolutionizing *pain-into-purpose*.

For the first time I felt free, alive, and overly anxious about living my life to its fullest potential. More than anything else, I owed it to me to learn how to love, and respect myself while taking control of my life.

As the fog lifted, my life slowly began to rebuild through my word-slinging as an idea architect, until an appallingly heinous invasion of my privacy, courtesy of the crowned—Pelicans Tellin' Porkies—left me bereft as they trifled with my free-fall into mental demise, like they were the rolling dice, betting I would crap out.

The deep-pocketed predators armed with unlimited resources, unleashed a campaign of psychological warfare, all because I boldly confronted these elite feudal lords who rule their small-town fiefdom.

The Pelican's revenge was criminal— a strategic assault on my sanity, with the driven intent to subdue my sentence sorcerer dreams as a metaphor whisperer.

It wasn't until they stumbled through the grapevine and learned of this memoir that they crossed every boundary imaginable to steal an illicit front-row seat into my private world.

Pelicans utilized advanced surveillance to hack into my life—listening, watching, and digging for proof to confirm if I violated a coerced NDA or not... it was *not*.

Overplaying their hand, the clumsy Pelicans—fueled by arrogance—dropped Freudian slips about my life, tipping me off to their unethical deeds as they exposed the depths of their machinations.

Intimate details of family conversations, digital diaries, and creative work could only have been ascertained through illegal and sophisticated spying on my home, devices, and my very existence.

When I opposed those involved, they retaliated with bloodthirsty gang-stalking, subjugating me with violent intimidation—

snap - p o p p i n - ' n ' - c r a c k i n '
my mental health, endowing me with the
lingering gift of PTSD.

These Pelicans, aided by fraudulent
companies masquerading as trustworthy
institutions, didn't just break laws—they're
shattering the very sense of security they
publicly profess to uphold within their
business models.

Locked, loaded, and armed with the
bare-knuckle truth, I am demolishing the
whole teapot in this power-packed book by
leaking their birth-tags. I will defy all odds
and deliver a fool's mate check to the
Pelicans—my triumphant counting coup.

Above all, this work is for *You*—for the
few who might find a spark of healing in
my raw, and unfiltered story. Or for the wit
chasers seeking a mind-spinning, turbulent
tango of words to lose themselves in, as they
maneuver through the uncharted depths of
my cognitive odyssey.

Either way, I am proof that redemption

and self-love is achievable. Even when life feels irrevocably mangled, and you have neither the strength nor the plan to move forward in the billowing time in question.

RTFUA is not some fluffy, sugar-coated memoir—it's unapologetically intense and brutally honest. An unfiltered replay of my life, crafted to meet the demands of the title—written for minds allergic to taking offense **(18+)**.

Adult themes, drug references, profanity, dark humor, and original metaphors that hit hard with audacious precision. All of it woven together with sharp truths disguised as 'conspiracies,' political satire, biting parody, and a heavy dose of sarcasm—challenging perceptions with authentic conviction.

Before we dive in, I pose this question: *"How can you begin to comprehend, judge, like or love someone for who they are... before understanding the wounds they've endured, the struggles survived, and the moral compass that guides them?*

What F*cked Me Up...

The front door squeaked open as my body went stiff, urging me to pause the video game. Unfortunately for me, listening to my intuition was never really an option.

Without wasting one second Pops yelled, *"Moniqie, come down and unload the car!"*

Given my alternate-universe priorities, there was a gaping delay before I shouted back, *"I will... once I finish this level in Super Mario!"*

The words barely left my mouth before I heard the Old Man stomping up the stairs as he huffed, and puffed, like a bull ready to charge. This level of heavy breathing was the soundtrack of his short fuse about to blow.

At that moment my inner dialogue whispered, *"I really should have paused my game and helped him."*

But there was no room in-thee-brain for logic when fingers-deep in the virtual world.

This adolescent thinker of mine was on autopilot, fully unguarded and oblivious to any ramifications—a green fairy cocktail fueling Pops' reckless, authoritarian mind f*ck.

Dad took all of three seconds to shatter my illusion like a dart popping a balloon at the fair as his bellow shook the walls.

*"What the f*ck did you just say to me? Do you think the world revolves around you, just like your mother? Get your ass up... RIGHT NOW!"*

Pops' second attention was jabbing his finger viciously in the air like an épée ready to fence-a-bout as his glare froze time.

Our eyes locked in a stifling eternity as the silence dwelt suffocating in the tension between us—invading every fiber of my being with nightmarish terror.

Without warning, the Old Man lunged toward me to warm the right side of my face,

8

with a backhanded strike to the cheek.

Before I could register what happened, he palmed the other side of my face. It was a crazed symphony of insanity by the 'Child Abuse Conductor.'

Shakily startled, I crumpled onto the shaggy carpet, stunned and motionless— the taste of shock, sharp in my mouth. It was like chewing on bitter melon doused with hellfire super-hot sauce.

Hovering over me, Dad's mug burned crimson with his veins throbbing like strobe lights.

"This is a dictatorship!" He howled. *"Not a democracy—not until you're eighteen!"*

To protect myself from his violent rage, I flung my hands up, only for Pops to thunder, *"Lower your hands! Stop crying! Or I'll give you something to cry about!"*

Hands-on parenting was well-deserved in his delusional mind. To stay on the Old Man's good side, I had to obey instantly, figure things out on my own, never screw around, and by no means make him repeat himself.

Every word from Dad's mouth was to be treated like gospel, and I was his unwilling disciple.

This thwack was anointed as my 'Most Memorable Hits.' It was the *bright-n-shiny day* that seared itself into my ten-year-old inner dominion as the first demeaning and indoctrinating slap to the jowl I ever internalized.

Back then, my snack-size-sapien's noodle was barely seasoned and still dripping wet. Inquisitively quick-witted, craving answers like the other juice-box junkies—driving me to vivaciously rehearse the instinctive rebuttals that plopped into my thought-pot.

Questioning everything meant it was all too easy for Dad to fly off the handle, especially with me. More than anything else, I reminded him of the woman who—in his distorted mind—*ruined* his life.

The exuberant amount of energy I

possessed, the way my eyes lit up at life, and my love for Mother Nature were all Mum's fingerprints—which he tried to erase as if covering up a crime scene.

Pops blamed me for her essence and his unhappiness—for everything. In simpler terms, I was his punching bag, undeniably.

Ever since I was a semi-dwarf apple tree, I had slowly grown spoiled. Ripening into Adam and Eve's rotten jewel, taking more than a bite out of the forbidden fruit of life.

Rarely was I afraid of anything—at least—not until the day Dad connected his hand to pulverize my cerebrum into applesauce.

The pressure to be at his absolute disposal started before I can remember. I only know this because the Old Man video tapped everything—*everything* I thought was supposed to be a nostalgic keepsake, that is.

Unsettling so, Dad's family recordings were not to create mementos but to script his own narrative. They were props in his endless courtroom drama with Mom for 'good-father' evidence.

These tribunal appearances only bled them both dry of money, while solidifying anyone who was involved to be miserably scathed. Daddio exhausted every scandalous option to prove a point or win against Mother in any way, no matter how trivial.

The video in which I was the youngest soaking in his toxic ways was from Easter, when he instructed a mere four-year-old to retrieve scissors and open huge, candy-filled baskets.

Heart-attack frustrated, he grumbled about the scissor delivery taking an *eternity*. Pops was sitting on the floor stuck in his impatient mode of a manic uproar, with no intention of getting his lazy ass up.

"Jesus Christ! What is taking you so long? The scissors, the scissors, they are in the kitchen drawer!" Pops clamored.

Instantaneously, the Old Man's stubborn brain processed his irrational behavior toward a toddler, and the fact that the camera was still rolling. Daddio caught live in the eye of truth, persuaded himself to switch over to a sweet, fatherly performance.

A façade that, though it flickered with hints of truth, it was something he wore consistently for anyone who might judge or heaven forbid—hold him accountable.

Alarmed enough to quit while he was behind, Pops redirected his attention to the sweet chocolate goodies he was about to open for his one-and-only, *angel.*

No matter how Dad's cookie crumbled, he operated under the assumption that I should withstand his hollering while displaying the common sense of an adult, regardless of how young I was.

About six years old is when spanking on the butt with his hand was introduced to me—a quick, tappy-tap—enough brutishness to reveal if I was goofy or regular.

Around eight, the Old Man asked me if I wanted a thin or thick belt. I clumsily alleged the slim strap would inflict the least discomfort—wildly inaccurate.

Waiting for the first whip was always a nail-biter since I could not see anything. I would lie belly-to-bed, arms stretched above me with my shoulders pressed to my ears—trying to shield my face and block any misses, bracing myself for each lash.

That hot, prickly, and stinging after-feel carved its verdict—next time, thick-it-is.

Although the-Pops accredited himself to be well-versed, he sucked at whipping a belt.

The Old Man's wrist-snapping, mis-aimed craze landed everywhere but my butt. When he connected with my heinie, it was paternal perfection at its peak.

Gladly, I would've taken the strap over a smack to the face any day, but once he got that adrenaline-relieving taste of hitting me in the face, it became his go-to reprimand—instinctive, immediate, and easily accessible.

At some point, I grew defiant enough to bob-and-weave to duck Dad's hits.

Almost like when I used to watch the UFC around 2006, there was a now popular podcaster who commented on MMA fights. Back then, his favorite word to describe a fighter always seemed to be *elusive*—that was me.

On the daily, Old Yeller swore with a boundless temper as if yelling was his default volume, and rage was the love language that fulfilled his measure.

Daddio and I had our own kind of father-daughter dance, not to be confused with the two-step or waltz.

Pops' blame game played overtime, and I was never benched. As my third-base coach he slap-hit home runs to his double trouble. Dad directed all of his hatred at me because he could not show the crowd how much he truly despised the world.

To some degree, the Old Man knew how despicable it was to be this out of hand all the time, but his temper overtook any level of emotional intelligence.

Somewhere deep down within the Old Man he carried contrition that occasionally breached the rippling descent of his ego, albeit fleetingly.

Given that I was so used to Old Yeller's daily rants about this, that, and whoever, after a while, I did not jump up *on-the-double* to get the job done that was asked of me.

Whichever of his busted obstacle courses I decided to race on, something I did not foresee, always bungled me up to cause an undesirable outcome.

The rite of passage into an innocent and safe childhood was hijacked during my Most-Memorable-Hits. It was a dazzle-burst of brutal strikes that robbed me of a pure life.

This disastrous display of 'keeping-me-in-line' never left me to be the same. A light flipped on or off in my cranium cracker after feeling that escalated blood flow, skedaddle through my face.

All that clobbering and daily degrading incubated the naughty devil-girl that was slowly creepin' within me.

Reflecting now, I tried to compare my current feels to what I thought in those soul-crushing episodes, and besides being dumbfounded—*I-have-nothing*.

Giant-fat goose eggs come to mind. There is nothing that would have delivered justice to my oncoming wreck of a mentality.

My free-range spirit was shoved into a cage with the key thrown away. This little duckling was about to be force-fed adult pain because of the sparkling glow that lit-up Mom's eye's—he saw in me.

Although Mother narrowly escaped the coop, over his dead body would he let other chicks slide through his wings, dismantling the power and control he so desperately needed over the family.

The Old Man's pigheadedness to be in command over the totality of us all, did not matter to me one iota. Once an opportunity emerged, I wasted no time for retribution, now that I was dead set on having an upper hand with Pops—in one way or another.

My first indiscretion broke the seal for a wide variety of shenanigans to come. As I ventured into cheap thrills, my schemes cascaded my decision making into a wild, out-of-control, cataract.

Bearing in mind that I was still wet behind the ears, I frivolously counted my eggs a bit too soon for that victory dance. I blocked myself in my tracks with an *"I know everything attitude"*—only to be wholly humbled by an *"I know nothing punishment."*

My first notable enormity took place when one of Dad's friends came down from the Sacramento area for a visit. A rare occasion that brought Pops' best behavior to the forefront of his cortex-catapult.

We were all headed to Lyons for dinner, which back then was a California staple chain founded in 1952—almost like a high-end Denny's.

I remember being annoyed with Fahzja, so, logically, I fired back with a witty, sarcastic one-liner to incite the feathers he loved to preen. My defiant experiment to turn the tables in our little pain-parade.

At the same time, I recognized the Old Man's reluctance to strike me in front of his buddy since he was a righteous man.

Within seconds of chucking my word throwing stars, Pops uncoiled like a whip to remind me who the boss was.

Classic dictatorship move—an unhinged scare tactic into submission to wring out a drip of respect he never *fully* earned.

Once Dad punctured thy personal bubble, my first instinct was pure survival—a quick jab to his gut with my wee-wittle fist-of-fury.

BREAKING NEWS: Monique's tiny hands were still coloring Care Bears with crayons—she was unable to stay within her lines. Sending the Chief Parent Officer into a foaming-at-the-mouth... *frenzy*.

In the natural order of chaos, my little stunt proved to be a full-throttle flop as Pops turned lava-red.

The Old Man was livid at my pathetic attempt to deflate his fecal-impacted, food baby belly.

Pops activated his rule-by-fear reflex and strong-armed his little provocateur into the corner for a timeout while they all feasted in unison, chewing in hypocrisy without their little wild-card.

This-here nose negotiated with the lead paint on the wall as my blood boiled. Stewing in my tanked crusade while I waited for Dad's beloved 1966 GTO to let out its smug purr and peeled out of the driveway.

Initially, I was ticked off that my daydream of pancakes for dinner had been banished by my own hand, leaving me home alone. But then it dawned on me—I could do whatever I wanted.

With a quick hop on the kitchen counter, I grabbed a gigantic cereal box and a huge baking bowl, ready to dive into a mountain of fruity-sugary bliss to silence my hunger pangs.

It was time for a quick bite and a video game session before Dad or the hosted demon encroaching within him returned.

Eventually, the original muscle—street GOAT—rolled into the driveway with its unmistakable purr, leaving me hotly startled. I hastily ditched my dishes in the washer, raced back to the corner, and bookmarked my nose into the wall.

Father's footsteps creaked up the stairs as my muscles clenched and cramped into a cringe-worthy place.

My goosebumps stood at attention as soon as the Old Man loomed behind me— armed with a silent presence that dared me to flinch, turn, or breathe wrong without his sacred, tyrannical walking papers.

The suspense was unbearable. Would I be getting the classic nonverbal shrug-off? Or the awkward, all-is-forgiven smirk?

What if he was still fuming? Would he serve me another spoonful of his bitter, tainted-life medicine?

On edge, my toes stretched and bounced slightly as I waited to be released from my invisible jailhouse shackles. Freedom was just one word away, but it was a lifetime out of reach.

Then, in a slow—hesitant voice—he would say, *"Okie... dokie... Moniqie."* This was his green-light, furtive-mutter that signaled to me that it was officially my yard time.

At last, I was free to invisibly roam our middle class pastures like a cow through an open field. Each step I took whispered to Mother Earth beneath my feet of all the pain... I-felt-inside.

There were no heartfelt talks, no warm exchanges, just the hum of nonchalance— like an endangered Florida Grasshopper Sparrow with its wings clipped, trapped in captivity.

After this bout, though, we started to see box office *hits* featuring dysfunctional, father-daughter thrillers. The kind with the emotional nuance of a disaster movie, where you want to pause and check if it's based on a true story.

Flashback to an ancient time when Pops boasted of being a ladies' man, long before I was ever a twinkle in his eye—let us be real... a tax write-off.

Picture this: white bell bottoms with a sewn-in Playboy bunny on the back tush pocket, courtesy of a local tailor to enhance the Old Man's strut while he showboated his peacock feathers as he ingratiated himself, gallivanting around *The Playboy Club* in San Francisco—hoping the freshly blossomed bunnies would take notice.

In the way of all things, his outfit in 1967 was not complete without an unlit ciggie dangling from his lips. It was the final touch to his charm-and-dance act as a tar-toting smooth operator, boogie-woogie-ing across the dance floor, leaving the chicks' hearts fluttering.

Since I was a sapling, smoking indoors was still permitted, which granted me the enforced prerogative to smell-like-a-walking *ashtray*.

This stale, cinder-receptacle aroma was my typical scent until I drenched myself in Peabody, Love-Spelled, and vanilla-musk body sprays to mask my reeked existence.

Pops, depending on his mood, averaged about a pack of tar-tubes a day, give or take. He drooped a lung-rocket from his mouth all day whether it was lit or not—like a peculiar homage to puff-pioneer endurance.

The Old Man inhaled the smoke inside the house, car, palate playgrounds—wherever and whenever, I should say.

Of course, we always sat in the smoking section at flavor parlors while eating. Why half commit to a debauchery way of living, when you could go full throttle?

I hated it—*shockingly*—no big twist there.

No matter how smothering the hot-boxing intensified, I knew better than to waste my dwindling supply of pleas on something as trivial as fresh air so that I could breathe.

There was no way for me to know when I would need to use my next cry of *"I'm sorry, please don't hit me,"* with my puppy dog eyes aiming to pacify the beast within.

After all, those nic-sticks were his sacred ritual that calmed-him-down, a claim so preposterous it could have been a punchline.

Meanwhile, Pops was killin' it by racking up '5 Miles' from his branded chemical crutch.

For the uninitiated, these were thick tabs the smoke-stack-sapiens hoarded and tucked away until the prized redemption day.

Dad meticulously monitored his stash that were safe in his room till it was time to mail them in for the ultimate treasure—hype gear from the...

Cancer dies with you, our profit is forever catalog. From your first puff to your final bill—we feed your habits for cash... because freedom isn't free, but addiction is forever.

Nothing screams *peak* lifestyle like the Marlboro, coughing-cowboy crumbs you earned while slowly massacring your lungs.

Daddio's hawk eyes targeted unsuspecting smokers loitering in the public domain, huffy-puffing on their tuh-backie. He stared at them intensely, like it was a high-roller poker game, hoping to lock eyes and crack open that conversational door.

When the moment arrived, the Old Man swooped in with all the charm of a used car salesman, as he casually asked if the fumers were loyal to their brand. All in the hopes for Pops to finagle some miles for his own personal collection.

Problem was—most of these nicotine enthusiasts were just as devout about their rewards as he was. The tobacco-trailblazers had already peeled off their miles the moment they cracked open a fresh pack.

Why waste all that hard-earned lung capacity without something tangible to show for it?

In the world of nicotine-bound chaps, priorities meant branded swag as a return on investment, not a functioning respiratory system. Once we had amassed enough miles to order from the lung-bandit inventory, it was a free-for-all on what to select.

Predictably enough, I had first dibs and usually got whatever I wanted—provided it wasn't one of the costly items that were a few thousand miles out of reach.

The Old Man quickly vetoed with his sharp, *"We will never get that high!"*

My Camel's competitor swag was worn with pride: shirts, hats—I even a backpack or some bag I slogged around at school. Nobody else had this *exclusive* gear, and whatever it was, I strived to stand out differently than the rest, for better or worse. Even if that meant strutting around like a walking cigarette ad, so be it.

After years of watching the Old Man puff away like a chimney, the time had struck to see what the anxiety-soothing fuss was with the smokes.

27

After my *Most Memorable Hits,* late in fifth grade, I began plotting my first notch on the belt by activating the train-wreck tradition of *"I'm about to make some poor life choices... wanna watch?"*

In true glory seeker fashion, I deployed a stage-one trial in the 'How Will this Make Me Feel' research department. That way, I could study how much of a disaster in motion, and beautiful mess I could be.

Like a robber scoping a house, I moved with precision, peering behind different walls for better sight lines on the Old Man's whereabouts, until he left our maladjusted compound.

Lucky for me—if you could call it that— Dad was a master hoarder of his nicotine stash. He stockpiled the smokes to guarantee he would never face the apocalyptic horror of running out.

Sly-as-sin, I crept into Pops' cave and sticky-fingered a box of Virginia leaves and firepower.

Stealth mode was the next mission-critical step to verify if anyone was orbiting the house. I scouted for any uncalled eyes to stay unsuspecting of the monkey business I was about to swing into.

This-here-brain worked in overtime to cover my tracks like a true delinquent in training. As my heart pounded out of my chest, I became hyper-focused on coming out unblemished in my endeavor.

Before venturing outside to commit my dirty deed, I plotted out a foolproof plan to save time and minimize exposure.

Only a simpleton would fumble with the plastic and tinfoil packaging of the huff-sticks out in the open—bent over, utterly distracted, practically begging to be caught red-handed.

This was no amateur hour. Every move was calculated, smooth, and above all, undetectable.

Before stepping into the great outdoors for my first major bout of juvenile rebellion, I carefully unfastened the cigarette box as if it were the cure to my preteen existential crisis.

Smooth as a spy ditching admissible proof of a crime, I clutched the crumpled outer layers in one hand and tossed them into the trash. I was now fully geared up to head toward the most wayward, hidden corner of our yard to commit my petty crime.

Once outside, I crouched between the backyard bushes. My hiding spot oozed of elegance, like that of a feral kitty cat.

In a lickety-split fashion, I flashed my peepers down and carefully selected a stogie precisely from the middle—right where my logic dictated that my luck was stored.

As I gently pulled out my prize, I stared at it like it was magical. Glowing with the promise that all my conundrums would vanish in the blink of an eye, now that the Marlboro Messiah had arrived to save me from my own mediocrity.

Reaching into my jeans pocket, I whipped out Dad's National Airlines flip lighter as I said to myself, *"I did it. I finally did it and didn't get caught!"*

With the grace of a wide-eyed, untried whippersnapper, I flicked that sparker until a flame held steady, and the lighter fluid aroma filled the air like a victory dance.

Mesmerized by this flare, I mused at the last time I was unsupervised with a fire starter. An occasion that nearly culminated into a self-cremation close encounter.

Zoned out, my short-lived irreproachable smile turned to entertained by roguery when our near-death misadventure came to mind.

True to form, this narrow escape was at the top of Dad's list of cherished stories to tell, *repeatedly.* The Old Man loved to recount the illustrious day when his pyro-prone child almost turned everyone into a residential wildfire.

Highly intrigued, Pops would call me over whenever his eagle eyes spotted a loose string hanging from my clothes.

With a flair for the dramatic, he would reach into his collared shirt pocket, whip out his lighter like a legend preparing to make history, and ceremoniously burned the offending thread dangling from my shirt's base.

Pretty young during this preheated phase of life, probably first grade. Young enough to graphically narrate the day in question. A time when a fire igniter decided to cross my path as it whispered my name with the seductive allure of a forbidden toy.

The phrase in my inner-nutter would have been something along the lines of... *"Today's the day to blitz some strings, just like Daddy does. Game on!"*

At a tender, untested age, I inadvertently appointed myself the sole executor to exterminate every loose end in my world. Goes without saying, metaphorically of course.

There was no oversight committee, no second opinions. Just me and my newfound arsonist-ambitions, determined to rid myself of the burden of frayed threads. Because nothing screams independence like wielding fire at around seven-years-old.

This day in question was near a holiday when a mini-flamethrower found its way into my possession, and the possibilities suddenly felt *endless.*

Unfortunately, the likelihood that my combustive escapades were about to go public in one of the least flattering ways was also an option on the table.

Dad was stationed at the kitchen table with two of his cronies shooting the shit, acting like they were solving the world's problems.

This fact left me with scarce options, especially since one bedroom was already occupied.

Taking my time, I scouted for a secure location. Somewhere far enough from the baby boomers and the kindred spirits to sanctify this solo-expedition.

No way I would leave myself vulnerable to tattle-tellers itching to *grass-me-up* if given the chance. A pause was taken so I could autodidact my way through what I had deduced as rudimentary competencies.

As sure as the sunrise, kids should not play with fire—especially unsupervised—but honestly, how else am I supposed to learn?

Following the rules never entertained my headspace—and—when boredom sets in, I am wired to create new material to tame my neural dance.

So... with reckless optimism, I made the call that Pops' cave was the perfect venue for my firebug debut.

In a silent shuffle, I cautiously cat-crawled inside, my eyes darting as they hunted for my targets. Only to discover tantalizing strings dangling beneath the Old Man's bed.

Jackpot.

The first stringy victim I honed in on was slightly tattered, curled, and attached to the mattress box. I vividly recall the giddiness of lighting it up and pulling it off, watching it smolder for a moment before fading into ash.

Finding a few more here and there, I incinerated them posthaste with my trusty heat genie. By the third or fourth string, the novelty had already worn off.

Easy victories made my adrenaline take a deep dive as if I was sprayed with mono-ammonium phosphate—on the brink of relieving me of my pyrotechnics.

This mind-blown elation I anticipated was a bit of a stretch—not quite panning out as I had envisioned. So, I moved onto the strings on the blankets, hoping to spark-up a *wittle* more excitement.

But then—**POOF**—a baby fire kindled.

No clue where it came from—the mattress box, maybe?

Full-tilt into a hysterical freak-out, all I could do was aggressively blow on it, as if it were forty-two birthday candles about to set fire to Mom's sky-high, aerosol-sprayed hair in 1984.

This-here thought-engine assumed it would disappear just as quickly, and with the bare knowledge I encompassed, it made sense.

BIG... *mistake.* The flames responded instantaneously by expanding as if to say *"Nice try, rookie."*

In an emergency overdrive with zero desire to explain myself to anyone, my logic lump officially clocked out. Now left to my own devices, I transitioned into fight mode.

In a blur of desperation, I pogo-sticked my scrawny legs onto the kitchen counter and grabbed liquid holders to fill with water.

My grand plan?

Rubber-stamp my makeshift firefighting skills and hope for the best. If it worked, I would celebrate my victory in silence. If it didn't... the fallout would be dealt with later when I had no other alternatives.

Dad and his buddies glanced at me with mild curiosity as I darted past them to snatch up some cups. Their faces asked, *"What is this kid up to now?"* But not enough concern to interrupt their sacred ritual of chewing the fat.

After the chums finished processing my *harmless* reach for slurp vessels, they effortlessly shrugged me off and went right back to their conversation.

Fiasco averted—*for now.*

Briskly running to fill the sippers, I tossed the water onto this energy-efficient, heating solution—but not a dent was made.

My young brain knew I had to suck it up and summon adult reinforcements. The time had come to fess up and take what was coming to me. This realization hit me like a blue-ringed octopus bite—instant hysteria, with deadly consequences *if* I hesitated.

Time to brace myself as I was about to test Pops' no-anger-management soil by digging up his temperament. Ensuring his 9.5-earthquake-like temper loosened, bubbling up into a catastrophic aftershock of attitude.

Growing up around controlled burns, I understood the seriousness of our current predicament. Add to the fact that we were on the second floor of a townhouse, connected to two other homes with kids, no less—and suddenly, the fire was not just *our* problem.

It was prep talk time to rehearse my game plan. A strategy to summon the courage to concede that this rapidly expanding fire was no longer viable for me to handle on my own.

So, I quickly tossed the glasses to the floor and bolted as if jolted by a round of electric shock therapy. All while informing the bootlickers about the eco-smart heating setup I had uncovered.

Taking a wild stab that this was the admission of guilt that looped endlessly in my head... *"I am so dead for this."*

"Daddy, I have something important to tell you—but—you have to promise not to get mad at me first" as I looked up at him, trying to turn on my 'I-am-too-adorable-to-yell-at—bambi eyes.'

His voice laced with unease, sharpened as he demanded, *"Tell me what it is, Moniqie!"*

Doubling down on my negotiation tactics, I shot back, *"No, no... You have to promise first."*

Dad barked with his tone shifting into full-blown authority mode, *"Moniqie, tell me right now—or I will get mad!"*

"Okay! Your bed is on fire!" I yelped, my voice shooting up an octave.

"What?!" Dad roared as he slammed his hands down, and jumped up like an outlaw about to flee the Blue Meanies.

All three lackeys ran into his bedroom shouting over each other like the Three Stooges, on fire themselves. One guy grabbed a five-gallon laundry bucket we would get from a wholesale store, dumped out the granular soap onto the carpet, and filled it with water from the tub.

'Moe-Diculous,' aka the Old Man, frantically searched for a fire extinguisher while the other made do with bowls of water.

Somewhere in the madness the fire department was called. This happened late in the afternoon, and Dad swore I somehow managed to fall asleep amidst the chaos.

Apparently, I was extremely-exhausted from the *trying* circumstances. I beg to differ and argue it was more the emotional toll of *saving-the-day,* but sure, let us go with the former.

People darted in and out while Pops yelled and panicked for our safety. I, on the other hand, was calm as a pond on a windless day, fatigued by their *overreaction.*

I mean, *really*—where's the calamity? The amateur fire brigades had the dancing embers under control as if there were no learning curve—the blazin' heat was subdued rather quickly, all things are considered.

The only damage was to the bedding, mattress, carpet, and every-single-one of Pops' safe keeping treasures, which he stored under his bed to be protected until the end-of-time.

Evidently, the next morning, I strolled into the living room with the audacity of a kid who hadn't just set a mattress ablaze and threatened the lives of others.

Stretching my arms wide with a dramatic yawn, I rubbed it in, *"I slept soooo well last night—Daddy!"*

"Don't push it, Moniqie..." he mumbled.

The Old Man was sprawled out on the couch like he had just survived a natural disaster. He was still fried from the previous night's festivities, with a tone hinting at resentment.

Surprisingly, I was never yelled at or chastised for my burning-the-bed ritual.

Dad, however, instructed me to avoid playing with fire. A lesson he articulated with flawless, diamond-cut clarity—much like the truth which can endure any pressure.

Naked-facts and lustrous-carats deserve to be seen from every angle, in every light, and I will not sparkle for anything less.

Back to the nicotine-fueled juncture where I began—bit-by-bit—belligerently launching friendly fire at myself, thanks to my pryingly rebellious ways.

Only to instigate myself to uncover every absurd possibility of how to torpedo my own vessel into enemy territories, thanks to the ghastly choices I made.

This all caused me to quietly tuck away a fathomless, intrinsic melancholy, forcing me to chirp inwardly—unlike a hermit thrush—as I tried to translate my own song of life.

Reality eventually came knocking when Dad's silver flip-lighter heated up in my hand, cueing me to abruptly jam the lucky stogie between my lips—spark it, and inhale deep—only to be seized by an aggressive, choking cough. I then deliberated on how anyone turned to smoking to ease their nerves.

Suddenly, I realized I had been outside too long. The clock was ticking as I pictured Pops barreling down like a sledgehammer. A collision I refrained from inviting.

I double-timed it to the garage to bury the brand new pack of cigarettes at the bottom of the garbage can, well out of sight—hidden within the folds of neighborly trash.

Then, it was time to put on a show. To role-play like I hadn't just gotten myself into mischief. But first, I had to return the Old Man's prized, vintage-style lighter to the exact position where he had left it.

This tally on the scorecard, botched smoking getaway, took place at the end of fifth grade, just before the summer leading to sixth. It was around the same time Pops started spending more time with someone new—or maybe I was just then meeting her.

Transforming into Dad's disorderly fixture wherever he went—like a cuckoo clock, chirping off-key and always an hour late— suggested that it was too high of a risk to leave me home alone.

The friend's name was Judy, and she was quite a bit older than Pops, while on the real-good-stuff... *painkillers*, if you know what I mean.

Judy's abundant collection of 'scripts' took away her suffering from cancer. On the instant, her euphoric sentiment piqued my interest.

I was tired of my alley cat attitude: always on edge, back arched, claws out, ready to hiss or scratch up anything that got too close.

Her calmness was like an oasis, and for a moment, I wondered if her solution could quiet my chaos too.

Every time I was at her place, I glanced around to find which bottles looked the fullest. Once the coast was clear, I covertly swiped one or two pills from each.

The first time I knocked one back, it had me flying so high—in complete bliss—that I fell straight asleep.

After this zonked-out session, I decided to get strategic by splitting the opiates in two, that way I could stay awake and savor these beaming sensations. But to my dismay, this off-the-cuff, frugal dosing experiment with narcotics was unsustainable.

This stingy, child's-play serving failed to deliver the goods that I promised to my mesolimbic system. My pleasure network was beyond disappointed—it was straight-up, struck-hard with offense.

Given that half-asked, measly, entry-level dosage, I stepped up my game from the dabbler serving by increasing and mixing it with other remedies.

At some point, word got out.

A friend—or maybe some kids at school—sussed-out my access to this coveted good stuff, and suddenly, they were *in-like-flynn*.

Pathetically, it was as if I were the new cool kid since they came excitely to me for something. A fleeting moment as if I were liked or being accepted for once.

There was a unique children's song that was viscerally ingrained in my mind, one I would sing whenever I felt like a pariah at school: *"Guess I'll go eat worms... big-fat juicy ones, itty-bitty bitsy-ones—time to shove my head in the dirt to hide what I can't undo."*

Don't hold me to the verbiage, I might have ad-libbed to drop me a bit lower.

All the same, I was quite favored in my situation, given that Dad's friend had an ample supply of pills and seemingly did not keep track.

At least, that's what I concluded at the time since I began to take full bottles, and nobody batted-an-eye or questioned if my phalanges had bypassed child safety protocols and approvals.

This cloud-nine phenomenon wasn't just a high—it was a blind-pressed bet where I willingly anted up against myself to see how far I could spiral into this self-sculpted-hell.

Already in deep as the big blind, I chased even more losses by sneaking out of the house. Other times, I let older peeps tiptoe into my room through the back driveway's convenient access.

These dodgy youngsters were a mixed bag. Some barely-of-age adults, all trapped in an unremitting state of adolescence. A motley crew of bad examples, united by the shared goal of going all or nothing—living life on borrowed time—just like me.

Sampling drugs was like flipping TV channels with the delightful connections I made. My loyalty went to pain pills, Valium, alcohol, and cocaine. Mollies, the Mary Jane, shrooms, and LSD got their fair share of my devotion, *too.*

A twisted Chef's tasting menu that was coursed out with blitzed ingestibles—never one to turn down a complimentary course.

Daily vilification and constant face-taps were like tampered Halloween candy with razor blades shredding me up on the inside.

Over time, my emotions and nervous system numbed out as if I ingested a spiked cocktail with thallous chloride.

The ole' tear ducts were despondent for being left out in the lurch. They quickly followed suit, drying up like when calcium chloride takes on ether.

Pops knocked the sensibilities out of my being, molding my monotone face—perfect for having a bash with cards, taunting my lady luck, but useless for any meaningful relationship.

Whatever those sensitive-feelings are that people talk about, I was never privy to rule them in or out.

Narcotics and alcohol—my go-to coping mechanisms, never once did me the courtesy of silencing my insecurities. If anything, they were amplified by over-analyzing every instant—no matter the standing—until my brain tapped out for mercy.

Never to delve deep enough to implement anything constructive. Why bother when self-destruction was my safe, at-home space?

I did, however, tap into my lack of faith in myself by constantly asking, *"What is wrong with me? Why am I never accepted? What did I do to become a blobfish that makes people lose their appetite?"*

With Dad, it was like I was the unwanted stepchild he was stuck keeping an eye on out of sheer obligation. Still, to his credit, he had my back in certain situations, like when I got suspended for fighting.

This one time—at school—I had my first dukes-up moment, back in the sixth grade, with a last-minute sparring partner.

'Reen,' a so-called *fwiend* who had been to my house, spewed insider gossip about my family—her duplicity sharp enough to draw blood down my face.

A solid portion of misfits spit-balled wildly differentiated scenarios about what was about to go down—their wickedly-sharp solution?

Fisticuffs—a fight to settle the score. Of course, that plan was agreed upon without my input.

When the final school bell rang, we were to meet at the dividing line between the park and the community center—far enough from school enforcers and parents during pick-up time.

Skipping the last class, I headed over early with a small group of kids so I could be the first one there to plan it all out. I hated surprises and needed the extra time to think, especially since I would see her coming.

From a distance I spotted a few guys, seemingly high schoolers, dawdling about. I did not know them personally but pegged them as the neighborhood hoodlums I saw regularly as we rubbed elbows enough on the block.

Millbrae, a town with basically no crime back then, was home to our urban, wannabe street gangstas. I would wager these cosplay thugs never circled the concrete jungle or committed oops-with-intent worthy of an iron-bar retreat.

When I reached our Lincoln Circle Park, I hurry-scurried up the little hill for a better vantage point. I wanted to scope out the area in case any curveballs were thrown—and admittedly, to say hi to the hooligans.

Fittingly, making small-talk with fake,

tough-guy energy would be the perfect warm up before my scheduled brawl.

As soon as I reached the top of the hill, one of them holla'd, *"Wassup, Monique? What are you doing here?"*

I remember being candidly surprised that they even knew my name. Without missing a beat I blurted out, *"About to be in a fight, it looks like."*

Now, feeling a little jumpy and alert as heck, all I wanted to do was end Reen with a quick, *"Wham-bam, but no thank you!"* That way we would be on our opposing ways at breakneck speed.

Nearly forgetting why I was even there in the first place, lost in the googly-eyed haze of smittenness—swept up by that youthful, swagger pulsing through the air, calling my hormones in ways unbeknown to me.

Be it thus or otherwise, I was immensely appreciated the activated tingles, until nervousness bombarded me with images of flailing sucker punches.

Not about to be caught off guard, I yanked my head around to the path I presumed Reen would be walking.

Sure enough, just in the nick-of-time, a swarm of young-ins started to make their way toward us. Figures that her crowd was vastly greater than mine.

Still, no energy was wasted on paying attention to her bee broods—they were fly over, aerial shit-starters, *only*.

They were not part of Reen's crew that would jump through hoi-polloi and trip over the curb to throw down if she were losing, ensuring I would be outnumbered to secure that... *victory*.

As Reen strutted, she spewed her best shit talking with each glide to sting my nerves, but there was no effect to be had on me. My eyes were on that honey pot—braggin' rights to not mess with me.

Our knuckle-tussle in the park was exactly what it needed to be:

One and done... Monique, WON.

Inspired by this reminisce, I added my own spin to a gamblin' saying, *"I knocked you blue—no wagyu dinner for you!"*

This baby crow was caw-cawing without making a sound. My wing feathers held her weight at bay, and I did all the work.

Reen was laid out on the ground, holding her jaw as she wiped my spit off her face. I proceeded to stand over her to savor that vision.

Throwing her hands up, Reen begged me not to punch her again. I then advised her never to have my family or my name come out of her mouth, again.

My adrenaline was bumpin', pumpin', and thumpin'. All I was twitchin' to do was— make-like-a-banana and... *split*.

Without further ado, I made my way through the crowd of *"Oh shit! No, she didn't"* reactions, to head downtown for some junk food before doubt could settle.

There's no way any doors would be left open for her more intimidating killer bees to swarm me if they flew in late.

Over the years, Reen's allies earned a certificate of non-completion in my knuckles of education. It never mattered if I was outnumbered or if the girls stacked up against me were triple my size—thanks to Dad's rigorous *training*.

To reward myself for a job-well-done, I treated myself to my favorite sweet treats, courtesy of the roll of laundry quarters I swiped from Dad's room.

Why bother Old Yeller for permission for quarters—the ones he complained about waiting in line at the bank for—when I can offer forgiveness at his convenience?

Unexpectedly, as I paid for these goodies, my pager buzzed in the front right pocket of my jeans, setting off a guilty conscience as my heart sank.

Zombified, I shuffled out of Walgreens, bracing myself as I pulled out my beeper to see who was summoning me—oh boy—Pops' code.

I freed the pager from my hand, letting it dangle from the cord. It swung back and forth like a disjointed hula hoop as I stood there frozen, mindlessly speechless. In a state of pure-paranoid-shock, convinced the Old Man somehow knew about the fight.

For the life of me, I could not figure out who snitched as barely two hours had passed. Pops generally left me alone unless I missed curfew or got caught with 'blood-on-the-blade' in some trickery.

Clutching the change I had left, I walked in crisis-mode to the nearest phone box. Feeding the coins into the payphone slot, I compelled my finger—against its will—to dial each number. I stood there, fully prepared for the Old Man to pick up on the first ring.

Dad's voice blasted through the receiver, hitting me like it was coming straight out of a megaphone, *"Where are you? The police are here looking for you! Get home so you can tell me what the hell is going on!"*

Words flew out of my mouth faster than

the hovering flight of a hummingbird's figure-eight wingbeat—flapping 77-times per second in the air as I rapidly fired off, *"I'm downtown... walking up now!"*

The archaic communication device was slammed on the hook as I snappily-snapped into action. In a true chop-chop fashion, I gave myself a quick once-over, ensuring I did not look disheveled.

Then, feeling like I was marching into deadly territory, I made my way back to the suburban streets to walk my cement plank. On this journey home, I played out every possible scenario in my head, each one more extra than the last.

In the end, my first house call from the Po-Po's terrified me far more than the Old Man or the fight itself.

By some stroke of divine timing, the Bizzies had departed before I arrived. Dad briefed me on my two-week suspension as I tried my damnedest not to smile.

Was this not a sweetly capricious turn of fate? No school with the home to myself and no watchful eyes in sight...

Sign. Me. Up.

Who knew rebel-esque antics would win me time off in the trouble-maker lottery.

Pops' slow smirk signaled I was in the clear, fully aware of my elation. He then confirmed that I was not *up-a-gum-tree* when he gave me a small, amused applause.

"You're lucky you were sticking up for the family, and not over something stupid. You can relax and smile."

Relieved and grinning ear-to-ear I asked, *"Can I go play video games now?"*

"Yes, Moniqie-mou, go have fun." He replied with an entertained look on his face.

In a flash, I bolted into the living room and tossed my backpack onto the floor. I was more than ready to get down to business to earn that purple thumb.

Close calls with the Five-O happened more than once, along with a healthy collection of school suspensions.

As if that weren't enough, by freshman year I was one sick day away from being expelled—or so they claimed. It must have been their scare tactic in response to my forged documents that came to light, with everything else I was up to.

Contriving fake records was not some innate talent I conjured up on my own. It would not be honorable to take all the glory for such exceptional work without naming the muse behind the mastery of my craft: Pops.

Dad was always on top of technology. When computers first came out, he had one and was perpetually fixated on it.

By the time I hit fifth grade, the Old Man acquired an electronic brain for me to dive into—after meeting his expectations on what I was to learn first, of course.

The primary skills on my Pops-assigned

curriculum were typing without looking at the keyboard, and to be literate in Corel DRAW to help design flyers for his business.

Even without the monetary incentives, I was intrinsically inspired to spare no labor in mastering the full monty—and then some.

It was also encouraging that I fervently loved the process. There was something fascinating about rapidly pushing buttons and formatting everything to satisfy my eyes' perception of *perfection*.

After I got the hang of things, Dad taught me how to compose a professionally typed letter. Then, as if gauging my budding prodigy status, he casually asked if I could sign his signature by looking at it.

Pops must have been measuring my eye-to-hand precision—or maybe it was because I was a quick study. I hemmed and hawed over what he was up to.

Either way, I followed his directions and signed his name. To this day, I remember his earnest-hearted laugh that was impressed by my version of his *John Hancock*—only to further fuel my newfound skills.

Once I mastered formatting letters, it was time to practice father's signature religiously. By the time I hit seventh grade, I promoted myself to write sick notes to excuse me from school.

In due course, Dad was early to pick me up from high school while in ninth grade. He marched straight to the office, weaponed with a legitimate letter to release me from class. That was the precise time he came face-to-face with the extent of my sick days, already taken off.

Let's just say given how early we were in the year, it did not look good.

Pops asked the school administrator for copies of the excuses he had allegedly generated, only to burst into a hearty cackle right there in the office. He chatted with the administrator while I stood there, officially, put-on-notice.

The second we were in the car, the Old

Man showed me my handiwork and seemed genuinely baffled when he said, *"I can't teach you anything... you take it way too far. You're too smart for your own good."*

Funny enough, Pops was beside himself and in a jolly good mood. There were no slaps, no yelling or harsh reprisals. It was almost as if he blamed himself for this one.

But, the fun did not last long.

Within weeks of my phony pardons coming to light, the Old Man escalated to alarming levels. This flash of hell came after I returned home from a party with two girls who were a grade ahead of me.

When I asked Pops for permission to go, he didn't press me about drinking or drugs. It might have registered as a trustworthy get-together. Or maybe he had given up— at least, that is what I had hoped for.

Truthfully, I was already steeped in tomfoolery and poppycock antics, like brewing high-potency, red kratom tea.

My routine consisted of 'going to bed' as

I stealthily slid out the back door without fluffing-the-air with words.

Only a handful of times had I ever asked for permission to go out. Reserving those rare requests for the perceived, *innocent* outings. That way I wasn't fully lying about my plans, just bending the truth a *smidgen*.

Early into the evening at this so-called *safe* shindig—I was, out of nowhere, hit with a wave of inner static I couldn't shake. Within a heartbeat, I was eager to find a ride back to my habitat, sensing my responsiveness weakening.

Within the first hour a couple of drinks were knocked back, but drunkenness was still far off. This was nothing like the personal elixirs that had already earned backyard approval.

No matter what the foreign substance, I was scared of this unexpected dose. We all hear stories about people slipping stuff into drinks, but I never thought it would ever happen to me, ever.

In hindsight, I should be thankful for this hard-earned tolerance and awareness. Built through my self-led medical exploration and trial-and-error in amateur *pharmacology.*

Silver-lining and all.

Recognizing something was wrong with me, I became chatter-powered to leave this underage extravaganza, scrambling to find a ride back to my base camp—faster than a caffeine-fueled cheetah chasing a rabbit.

As my mind and body began to fade, my besties arranged a ride back to my digs without delay. Fortunately, I lived only a few miles away and the night was still in its infancy.

All my angst melted away the moment I got into the car. I closed my eyes, leaned my head back, and foresaw myself curled up in soft blankets, fast asleep the second I walked through the door.

When I exited the car, I stumbled down the walkway with my keys in hand to save time.

Zig-zagging down the pathway, I bounced off the plants on the left that lined the walkway, only to overcompensate and collide with the fence on the right.

Rinse-and-repeat.

On my first attempt to unlock the front door, I grabbed the wrong nickel-brass dwelling opener, fumbled, and sent the whole set clattering to the floor—a jingle that echoed sharply, making me gasp in sheer agitation.

Before my breath could exhale my indignation, I was in a race with myself to get inside as quietly as possible before Pops' guard-dog instincts kicked in.

Frantically, I found the correct key and jammed it into the lock—like a drunk-'n'-horny man, ravenous to *get-it-on*.

Cue in the 'open sesame' incantation.

Overcome with relief for half a second, I glided through the doorway, inclined to fall into bed and sleep for a decade. But as it turned out, relaxing and crashing quicker than a raindrop-dropping, was a wildly incorrect assumption.

All that racket I caused outside had triggered Dad's finely-tuned, rottweiler vibes against intruders. I was not known to be early for curfew, and I still had a handful of hours before my homebound deadline.

Old Yeller with his signature-aggressive, booming voice, thundered down the stairs, *"Moniqie, is that you?!"*

This cranial command center was frozen in sheer delirium—frighteningly hesitant— once I detected his palpable displeasure.

Instinctively, I did what any cornered kid that was not in their right mind would do— ignored him, and careened straight to my room on the first floor.

Out of nowhere, I-felt-it—the weight of dreadful, sub-zero cold fingers of fright that gripped my heart.

It was the bull in the Old Man, breathing down my neck as he stood directly behind me. His presence alone sent a chill down my spine, inciting every baby hair to rise in petrifying horror.

Rotating around, I was met with his fiery scowl as he leaned in and roared, *"Why are your eyes... rolling back into your head?!"*

Timorous on what was about to transpire, I hooded my eyes, shrugged my shoulders, and tilted my head downward to avoid his piercing gaze—buying time to dig deep to find any shred of willpower I could call upon.

Once I managed to muster a vague trace of spunk, I muttered softly, *"I don't know. I wasn't feeling well and came home."*

Dad's response was swift and cutting, *"Are you doing drugs? Are there drugs in this house? What the f*ck did you take to make your eyes roll back? Tell me right now, Moniqie!"*

In dire need of solitude, I pleaded with him to leave me alone—spun around, turned my back on the Old Man, and wrestled with myself to make my way toward the bed.

That dismissal was like pulling the pin from a grenade as he imploded and exploded simultaneously. Pops' watchdog complex was unleashed, now duty-bound to assert his unmitigated power over me.

Pops put one hand on each of my shoulders, pushed me into the wall, and beat me like never before. Infuriated open palms that handed out blows, one-after-another. Pops pelted each side of my face—so f*cking hard—it made my vision black out and fade back in.

Given my half-hazed state, this might not be saying much. But he wasn't holding back one bit. It was unlike anything I had stomached before.

Embattled by fear and incapacitation, there was no way for me to even process a reaction to defend myself—not like me at all, especially at this point in my life.

Special thanks to whatever I was on for dulling the edge.

This here stupefied lassie flailed around

with no control until the Old Man grabbed both of my wrists, and shook me back and forth like a protein shake after a strenuous workout—fully inclined to bulldoze anything that crossed his path.

Like a bat out of hell, I hit the back of my head on the wall. Dad briefly stopped. My knees collapsed from the shock of it all— I was downright, ravaged.

From my root to branch, I was entirely too scared to open my eyes to get wind of what might happen next, and by no means did I want to infuriate Pops further.

It also seemed strikingly logical not to entice a game of peek-a-boo...

"Where are you? Ohh... there you are!"

Scrambling to hold my tears back under my breath, all I could produce was gasps for air, in-between my hyperventilated cries of brokenness.

Determined to stay oblivious, I held my ground to stay unaware of any last-minute, encore, whack-a-mole wallops the Old Man might impetuously liberate.

My mind was stunned that this happened to me. I never fathomed that Dad could take things to this level—ever. I was pitifully low.

The one time I wasn't running a ruse to do drugs on purpose, and came home like an *angelic* lambkin—this happened.

Suddenly, he snatched up my arms, clamped my pulse points and snarled, *"What the f*ck is wrong with you?"*

Only for him to aggressively release my wrists contemptuously downward, almost as if even touching me disgusted him.

In true dramatic fashion, the Old Man accelerated out of my room, denouncing the door behind him—a *fatherly,* 'man-up' performance. This was his penultimate act of a halfhearted boom.

The next thing I remember was waking up the following morning, still on the floor, exactly where he had left me—spiritless and drained.

No blanket. No help to bed. I was lying there—on the floor—like a pile of dirty clothes.

This drastic, trial-by-fire level of corporal punishment happened only once. And once, was plenty. It was the harmful turning point that spawned feeble tendencies.

Consumed by this wretched situation as if my hands and toes bore hangnails that suppurated into infected, swollen wounds, oozing yellowish-green pus from this grotesque mental contamination—a training ground rendering me useless.

Time to skip school for a few days. Not just because of the marks and bruises, I was an emotional wreck, with no interest in getting out of my bed or leaving my room.

Pops made no effort to talk to me after that... and I slighted him just the same.

Hiding in my boudoir, I only emerged when I was sure he had either left the nest or locked himself in his chamber. During these rare windows of opportunity, I would dash to the fridge to stock up on food and drinks for the day.

Thankfully, I had my own bathroom downstairs, which meant I didn't have to share it with anyone—a small blessing in an otherwise grim quagmire.

We spoke a few days later, but only for a valid note to submit to school. Without question, waking up on the floor was a significant turning point for me, certainly not in any favorable way.

This dark matter, cuddling session with the floor night, was the equivalent of an electric outage in my load center. This little transformer was incapable of regulating the voltages coursing through my wires.

After far too much delay, Mum was at last apprised of our impasse. We then devised a plan to be with her full-time. Although there was relief in knowing that arrangements were being put in place, I still attributed this excessive abuse to my silence.

For the longest time, I was conditioned to

believe getting hit was just part of the Dad experience. It wasn't until I laid out the full extent of what was happening that I saw how far from healthy and normal this was.

Mom already knew about the verbal tirades—those were impossible to hide—but she couldn't control his outbursts, let alone prove them in court when it mattered.

Every invocation she made to shed light on who Dad really was, failed spectacularly. So there I was, staying mute like a comic book by keeping all the whacks and smacks to myself—*silently*—in my head.

Waiting for the full transfer to Mom so I could leave Father's nest for good, I was handed an opening to assert my rights, but I ended up pissing the bed, royally.

Shortly after my abject cuddle with the floor, still in my first year of high school— I was in my room, hanging out with a friend.

Pops barged in, all fire and fury, barking at me to come outside. I told my then bosom-buddy to stay put, promising I would be right back.

Briskly running to the garage, I found Dad's friend 'James' perching next to a mammoth-sized cardboard box.

What was inside you ask?

Oh, just a canopy for parking cars. An assignment clearly screaming for my teenage expertise. Apparently, I was the fortunate soul that had been volun-told to assemble it—the whiz-kid that I was.

I stared at the box, then at the Old Man, and with all the sass I could access, I shot back, *"I am not building that. I have a friend over. I don't even have a car. Why can't you guys handle it without me?"*

Only for my comeback to ever-so-irritate Dad's pinched-nerve disposition, *"Who the f*ck do you think you are talking to?!"*

This wittle family project turned into a full-blown ordeal, one that made me squeal.

He single-handed his fore-handed to back-handed, leaving me branded and mentally stranded.

After Pops *knocked-some-sense* into me, I found myself laid out on the loose gravel of our rundown driveway. Pops stood over me, looming like he was gearing up for the next round. That's when James, a vastly larger man, ran over and pulled him off me.

The look on James' face said it all. Pure disgust at witnessing the Old Man lose control. Coupled with the disappointment of seeing Dad's lack of valor, and the unsettling recognition of his propensity to cross a line, no man should ever approach.

James was yet another sucker caught in Pops' fact-fudging. They both sat around and debated the origins of my delinquency.

What could possibly drive me to ditch class, drink, and dabble in drugs?

And perhaps the most pressing mystery— why was I sharpening my cheeky-tongue to a barb-wired, piercing point?

My attention turned toward the patio where my friend stood, staring with a mix of shock and startled ambivalence. Her survival instincts kicked in faster than a rumor in a small town.

Without a hint of hesitation she said, *"It's time for me to head home."*

And she did—just... that.

As time passed, James began to distance himself. It seemed as if witnessing the Old Man's abominable display of parenting left a sour taste in his mouth. He got the front-row seat to how not to treat your child, and apparently, James wanted no part of it.

When I returned to school after the *car-canopy* incident, I got an unwelcome summons from the counselor's office.

Upon walking in, I noticed the local Cozzer seated at a small table—a familiar face from around campus. He was also a sporadic shadow back in middle school. Uneasy about what was unfolding, I strolled over with an air of indifference.

"Come have a seat," the Jam Sandwich said in an even keel way.

Wasting no time, the Piggy-Wiggy Snort Donut got straight to the point and said, *"Anonymous information has been reported to the school, and I want to discuss what might be going on at home."*

Then, in comes the kicker, *"Has your father ever verbally abused or hit you?"*

My mind went blank. My soul shut down. As my brain silently hit the no, not-now button.

I was terrified. Not just of the Nickers getting involved, but of everyone finding out and for good reason.

In a shimmer of stardust, I relived the day Dad got popped—back when I was in first grade or so, only for him to be bailed out later that evening.

No shocker here, this wasn't exactly uncharted territory. The Old Man got swept up by the Wallopers for clocking our female roommate in the face during her brief stint with us.

This roomie was in front of Dad with her back to the wall where there was a unique wooden clock hanging. I stood to Pops' left and to her right. Our cohabitant's closest escape route was her bedroom to her left.

At the drop of a Wild Turkey 101 bottle, Pops struck her face on the left side as he slammed her against the wall. Without hesitation, she countered back by breaking free from his violent embrace to call the Mounties.

By the time the Rashers arrived, Pops was calm through guilt. He was fully aware that he messed up. I stuck to Dad's side like epoxy while he descended the stairs to open the door.

Condemnation spilled from the Old Man's eyes as he stepped out of the front entrance. He promptly put his hands behind his back while holding his head down as the Beat Cop moved in to cuff him.

One Badge stayed with me while the other Flatfoot escorted Dad to the car. By late that night, Pops picked me up from a house where I had been stashed.

When the Heat started to ask if any of this funny business was going on, my first instinct was to protect the Old Man. In conjunction with people finding out what he was doing to me, I was terrified of the fallout.

Although I partly understood the gravity of my situation, the Brass never explained what would happen once Daddy-Dearest was released, and knew full well why he was apprehended.

Plus, I had one foot out of Pops' door for permanent residency with Mom.

Not to mention, the Oinker didn't bother to explain the steps that would take place if the Filth actually did their job to validate these claims and arrest him.

There was no road map, no reassurance—only uncomfortable questions.

Granted, I did shoot the Fuzz down before he could even finish. Cutting him off mid-sentence, I flatly denied everything.

To give the Peeler a *brief* benefit of the doubt, I didn't give him a chance to explain what would come next.

Using what's been etched into my idea incubator, I can't brush aside the fact that the Beak Runner never questioned how a delinquent high schooler blatantly covered up for the accused father.

Did we forget the unidentified tip that came from James—my friend—or was it her mother?

One feasible scenario? The Tiggy was just going through the motions.

Let us not neglect this delightful layer in the disgustingly accurate truth in the saying, *"It would behoove you to have a few dirty friends in high places."*

Whatever the case may be, assuming things never left a good taste in my mouth—even after digesting someone's lip service and their hidden shadiness.

If this Blue Heeler had bothered to run

Dad's name, wouldn't his arrest record have come up?

By then, the Old Man had spent at least twenty-years in the smallish town, and possibly built connections with people who had tight-knit ties to the local Smokey.

Inspector-Gadget-of-Nothing-Ham, might have been influenced and encouraged to look the other way.

Hardly the first time, and unequivocally not the last, someone in an authoritarian position looked the other way to benefit one of their own.

Regardless of the mistreatment, I have no clue if I was ashamed to speak up or if it was because he was my father, and I loved him. I will never be sure.

Be that as it may, this balancing act of pretending I was okay, overflowed my being with a vexed sub-context. Leaving me hexed and perplexed while kneeling for healing, during these unrevealing dealings.

In the grip of it, I was strangely pacified that zilch came from my one-on-one with this Ticket Fairy.

Looking back, it's shocking that this Old Bill and other adults in these indispensable roles didn't take more cautionary steps to save an imperiled child in dire need.

Instead, this Millbrae-911 Super Trooper turned it into a game of touch-and-go...

I tried—she denied. Time to cut short any support and abort the police report.

Perhaps this is me talking shit or over analyzing, I guess. Or call me—*jaded.*

Provided that these life-endangering situations are taken more seriously now, that's what will matter at the end of the day— learn from history and do not repeat its mistakes.

For next time, they will not be blunders, but egregious agendas, serving some gain that is not availing to the adolescent.

Moving on to another slippery slope.

Besides Dad's yelling and hitting, he had a warped and appalling sense of humor. Most of his jokes are wildly out of line and racist, that they're unfit to repeat. Only one comes to mind that is even remotely acceptable for me to ink on paper.

When *Aunt Flow* first came to town, I was about eleven years old—Dad's response?

"Nobody should trust anything that bleeds for a week and doesn't die!"

As he casted off some hilarity-induced, body spasms for his hee-haw of boffolas, thoroughly entertained by his cleverness.

This preteen mind-meadow of mine could not discern how to process this so-called zinger. I had not yet had the chance to talk with Mom about periods, given that I was an early sprouted weed in the family—so my mind scrambled for clarity.

There was no rough draft saved in my neural network to assist with unpacking this awkward time.

Years later—out of nowhere, in my early

twenties—that period banter resurfaced in my cranial-circuitry.

My first thought? What a asshole thing to say to his daughter during a young girl's milestone.

But then, the deranged adult side of me kicked in, and I had to profess that it was comical. Time to scheme up some grade-A bullshit and squirrel it away in my funnies inventory for pool-hustlin' and shit-talkin' bar settings.

Moreover, I have some titillating gems crammed into my intro-spectacle, with other gut-splitting chortles about exes, whys, and all the otherwise.

Keeping these jokes to myself has been a challenge, but they're safely stored for a perfect moment when I can whip out my goods—or their anonymous-goods, I should say.

When all was said and done, Dad had my back when I should have been in significant trouble.

Yet, paradoxically, he rebuked me over the little things—moments that cried out for guidance, fatherly love, clear-sightedness, and a dash of emotional intelligence.

As improbable as it sounds, Dad was both an extraordinary father and an abysmal one in equal measure—a walking contradiction.

If the-Pops led by example with respect, patience and clear communication—what a different story we could have been, and an incredible thought to ponder.

Truth is, Dad lacked the psychological insight to make that choice due to his victim mentality, born from his childhood traumas.

The Old Man's battle scars of the soul leaked through his amygdala, corroding what remained of empathy and reason. Boiling into a viscous, corrosive seep that sizzled and smoked through him like hydrofluoric acid, eating silently from flesh to bone. Only for Fahzja to flick its frothing remnants onto anyone within arm's reach.

Daddio never loved or respected himself

enough to heal so that he could claim peace and prosperity. His convictions were either conscious or buried beneath denial, and they shaped him whether or not he ever engaged in a holy breath of purpose.

In addition, I see all the foolish things I did and the lies I told while Pops had my back—only to be proven wrong—time and time, again.

We created a rift never bridged, and a cycle that was never acknowledged to escape. Our walls were built from stubborn pride, and we called them boundaries—only to be haunted by the ghosts of our unloved selves.

No matter how hard I tried or didn't try, making it through a single day unscathed, was never in our cards.

Not to state the obvious, but of course I knew how to jam-a-stick in his gears, and did so, whether calculating or not. Stirring the cauldron came as naturally as becoming hungry and eating food.

The resemblance to Mom tipped the

scale like a bright red feather in a bull's nose, as it riled up an exasperated conniption fit.

Deep down, every fiber of my being resisted the truth: the long-standing war internally, where I loved and hated Dad in parallel strokes.

Pops' repressive instinct and need to keep me forever uncertain of where I stood with him, left me indecisive beyond cognition.

This underdeveloped iron will of mine bred instability amid our chaos-ridden dynamic, with the tension skyrocketing as time trudged on.

I didn't know how to make sense of the nonsense when we had the chance. Never to untangle the mess we called *family* before it was too late.

Stuck between these worlds, I am the one carrying the weight alone. Ostracizing myself on this earth until I can uncover the sacrosanct ways to grant myself mercy. That way I can convert my regrets into hard earned wisdom.

Because—*sadly*—we'll never know.

As certain as death and taxes—these bruised tendencies, disempowered mindset, and the looming shadows of my heart, churned within. Submerged fury erratically brewing, waiting for the worst moment to erupt and sloppily unleash my...

'Pandora's Box-of-Pain'

No need to patch things up or attempt to put Band-Aids on wounds that require reconstructive surgery.

Tapping into internal powers while facing personality demons head on will prove to be a priceless transformation. Once this darkness is transmuted into vitality through its acknowledgment and self-work, one will find themselves to be fortified beyond anything once imagined.

Yet, that kind of spiritual autonomy is never gentle—it unleashes destruction all at once—exacting a costly toll in a dramatic, hardcore fashion.

Between the molten wax of living, thy candle's flame endures. Dripping havoc that hardens into brittle layers, awaiting the hands patient enough to break, gather, and melt it down once more.

Poured and reformed, it rises toward an elevated state. And how one chooses to refashion that flame—setting a new wick, polishing the surface—summons the next incarnation of thy reclaimed light.

The Pain
I Felt Inside

Hurt was the intense pain I felt inside. It tasted like the salty tears that would stream down my face.

These afflictions were the lightning that struck me—feeding every known negative emotion to blow up in a mental storm, as it ceased any type of self-nurtured love and respect for me to embody.

Hurt is the color of bloody red.

It sounded like the screams I would hear over and over, in my head.

This radical, psychological devastation, dismantled my state of mind, leaving me abandoned in a dark confined place, with no way out on my own.

Hurt became a gut-wrenching stab in my back while I silently suffocated in a box around me.

The innocent maze of my mind...
was scattered-fractured,
into unrecognizable pieces.

This soul-shattering pain I felt inside,
utterly destroyed the core of my being.

Hurt blindly led me into
a downward spiral,
as it dragged me through
a misguided reality.

Almost costing me to breathe...
my very—last—breath.

Hurt was the heart-crushing pain,
embedded deep inside me.

Each day that I omitted my childhood traumas, my suffering intensified, feeding a relentless cycle that triggered a hopeless, and lifeless existence... to consume me.

Tellin' Porkies

"Oh look, mini horses in a huge sandbox!" I remember saying to myself, or maybe out loud. Only a few basic memories come to mind from this point in my life, being that I was only around six years old.

Stepping into a room brimming with childlike delights, I was introduced to a therapist with whom I would be spending the next hour or so with.

My world sharpened with excitement as my eyes locked on a mini-indoor sandbox, bang-on in the heart of the Behavior Babysitter's office.

An invitation to play in beachy-bits while surrounded by farm animals—the horses were my favorite. It almost felt like stepping into a heavenly realm, purely magical.

A hidden gem for kids, and the perfect way for the Stress Strategist to distract me from the real purpose of these visits.

This-here memory tends to crystallize around traumatizing situations, sadly. I am unsure if anyone explained why I had to be there.

What I do remember, though, is how much I enjoyed the visits. I felt safe. I didn't care about the questions being asked, or why I was even there in the first place.

This all occurred a good amount of time before the Old Man shattered me on my... *Most-Memorable-Hits*.

At this age, Dad's aggression and verbal abuse was mostly directed at others, although it often happened in front of me. While I was occasionally scolded and spanked with his hand, it hadn't escalated to anything too serious, just-yet.

In our case, the injustice system seemed to have the right idea back then by issuing a court order for an Emotional Plumber. I highly doubt judges were handing out couch confessionals like lollipops at a doctor's office, so someone must've seen a real need.

Not sure whether this Mental Tune-Up Specialist was recommended by name or if Dad found her on his own—Mom doesn't recall how we were all connected.

Honestly, I would have never given this Crisis Concierge a second thought, but around fifteen years after our sessions she reached out to me, and by then, I was in my early twenties.

This reunion was far from random. At the same time, it left a lasting impression—hot-branded onto my brain.

The Tangled-Tales Consultant noted that she was following up with past clients who had favorably destined the course of her career.

This Mood Manager beamed with pride as she handed me a copy of her book, co-authored with actual psychologists, of course.

She gleamingly explained that my family had earned its very own chapter. I rallied up the fakest enthusiasm I could manage to read about all the trauma that I spent a lifetime thus far suppressing.

Not one flimsy second was squandered on taking a glimpse of the insides. The resentment in me burned like a flame thrower projecting fire in combat.

How dare she achieve something built on the pain-I-felt-inside, while I was stuck imitating how happy people act, and that I was *not* a total train wreck.

After I processed the fact that we were studied and immortalized in an academic way—it was a bitch-slap to the face.

Naturally, her precious children's book was tossed into the back of my closet, right where it belonged.

A fitting spot, really. I was truly-hiding—not... truly-seeking. Avoiding all of life's fundamentals to keep from... truly-finding myself.

Dazedly exhausted from the day's events of acting the role, *"I am doing fantastic in life. Straight up killin' it... No, I am not another statistic that is succumbing to my demise."*

Rather than calling out my bluff-on-life, I gluttoned myself into a trance to feed my addictions—indulging in intoxicating drinks and coke-tails while chasing tail. Only to unveil a gushing stream of spiraled-out denial.

Then, Daddio *chose* to push up daisies, exposing this long-overdue declination of a world I had been clinging onto—like dog drool on literally, anything.

It wasn't until May 2020 that something reconverted my red and yellow marrow, activating stem cells within my medullary space, to properly kick-start my headfirst dive into unearthing the skeletons in my closet.

What better way to do a cognitive-autopsy to my scarred-outlook and martyr complex, than to reach out to this head-fixer-upper, who was behind the scenes before it evolved into depravity of maltreatment.

Curiosity swirled within—did she have notes, recordings or anything tangible from those sessions?

Something—*anything*—to help me piece together what in the good grief was going on with my tiny-tornado, think-a-torium.

Surely, if a whole chapter was written about us, there would have to be some scraps left behind. Plus, I was writing whatever this is turning out to be.

Her response, though, was—puzzling. No inquiries about Mom, only about the Old Man: *"I have fond memories of your father. He always had his heart in the right place loved and wanted the best..."*

Mom is fifteen years younger than Pops, safe to surmise she was still alive.

The Stress Whisperer's glaring omission of Mum in that social media message, left me feeling like the bedrock truths were not appropriately translated.

This dull response had me fully underway to crack open her—*groundbreaking*—child trauma book.

And once I did, the questions started piling up—how could she be so ill-advised?

For starters, in my opinion, this woman lacked the credentials or the basic ability to read between the lines and see things for what they actually were.

Once this Therapy Wrangler's *'ineptness'* to rescue me from child abuse burned itself out, I set her gaffes to simmer on the back burner, and moved from specimen to examiner. Letting her baffling, conceptual stance eases my nerves—if only a wittle.

Now, how did the Old Man come off so positively in her good graces?

Then it hit me... did they sleep together at any point in time?

Once I had evicted that gross brain splinter from my mind-melon, I worked on decoding how anyone could be erroneously misled by a mosaic of facts-'n'-lies being told.

That's when I reached a monumental discovery. An epiphany of astonishing, universal truths on how almost any situation can, and often does, devolve into mucked-up bull honkey.

CROCODILE SMILE THEORY:

Person One who casts lies upon Person Two—to all the looky-loos—inflicts an indecent taste in the shady spectators mouths. They all ban together to spread detrimental judgment not in favor of Person Two—leaving Person One as the *savior*.

The smear campaign of the century that leaves the unsuspecting Person Two looking like the ultimate ass, while Person One and the scandal-scavengers come out unscathed as 'innocent.'

Person One does not stop there—*oh... no.*

They kick things up a notch by setting elaborate traps to enlist a gaggle of nosy rubberneckers and busybody brigades, to spill the invented and manufactured tea they all orchestrated against Person Two.

Before you know it, Person Two is the star of a shady-slander they didn't even know was occurring, as Person One sits back and laughs in their ovalwank of slubberdeguillions and tattle-tailors.

Person Ones are cunningly snake-oiled—malevolently hornswoggled, and chicanery-riddled—bamboozling their hoodwinked and sharp-practiced minds, as they delude themselves into the illusion of win.

But, in reality, they're staining their souls deeper into the pandemonium pits.

All of Person Ones' underhanded scheming is merely an elaborate dance to save their own ass while on earth, by tripping up Person Two—an innocent life they are dismantling with ease.

When it's the Person Ones' time, their ill-fated soul will storm 666 mph toward a fake white candle that is high in the sky, fully convinced they are going to Heaven.

Turns out, they're barbarically absorbed in the Devil's dark-energy vortex, and violently yeeted down the fiery staircase to Hell.

Person One will not be living in Heaven for eternity with the Almighty God.

Congratulations, Person Ones!

Your evil ways on Earth, won you a one-way ticket to 'Infinity-of-Fire for Eternity.' Rumor has it, it's the hottest exhibition in the afterworld, personally curated by the Evil One himself.

Upon arrival in one of Hell's delightful layers—possibly Tartarus—Person One will receive their official 'Inferno Orientation.'

First item on the agenda?

To get a firm grip on Satan's inside-out pocket that is wedged between his flipped-over middle finger, pointer, and thumb.

The Devil holds it out for his bitches to grab, now that these Person Ones are fully lubed up and ready to go.

The Beast welcomes these Person Ones to the afterlife show, with Lucifer as their master and chaos will grow—cataclysm is shoved down in a venomous flow.

A-list dreams no more, soon they will see—their time as conformist socialists is but a broken decree—with the foisting of radical-feminism plus, is no longer a guiding esprit.

Then, the Fallen One drags them downtown to piddle-and-fiddle, adding belittles to every night's riddle. He'll diddle the diddlers, poke every spot—no inch or hole—will be left unsought.

The Devil twists and tears—grinds them into plight—a full-blown disaster with no end in sight.

Person Ones shapeshift into a black, cartoon-like soul with big-white ghost eyes and no mouth, imprisoning them to observe the Hell they created, incapacitated to say one-single-word to complain.

These screwed blips are now strapped to Satan's infamous pulley—lambasted into floating counterclockwise around their own lake-of-fire cage, subjugated by hate, and enslaved within walls that are engulfed in flames.

The tormentor is now tormented with extreme agony since they will always be at a consistent boiling point while mourning their morning, until later in the day when it really heats up.

Consigned to oblivion in their...

I - A M - B L E E D I N G You're - Tearing - Me - Up,

OWWIE-CELL.

Person Ones are left to dejectedly hover around and ruminate on the evil mayhem they inflicted. Never to adjust to their condemned abyss since that is the life after death they earned.

Before Person One's inevitable downfall, how do these unconscionable, would-have-been-aborted-by-their-mother... if-she-knew-how-they-would've-turned-out—sleep soundly?

How do they have the impudence to be proud of who they have become?

To top it off, Person Ones praise each other on their carefully executed toxic behaviors in a circle-jerk-of-Pelicans.

Elatedly boasting about their culpable liability in annihilating Person Two types—comparing notes to verify that they're all inflicting irreparable devastation at every facet.

Nobody should ever have to endure or tolerate a Person One with their viciously savage, egotistically driven, cruel and crass—ethos.

To put it lightly, it is quite disturbingly impactful to undergo this level of double-dealing.

Like I always say...

Some only see the side that suits their ego—zig-zagging the scenario to skew others' visions. Seeing both sides requires integrity.

Something Person Ones conveniently forfeit in themselves, yet they expect in others, without exceptions.

Royal Hell

Fading in and out of consciousness, I utterly lacked the ability to hold a single notion in my head. I could feel that I was curled up on a couch, halfway naked, positioned by a giant window as the sun pierced my eyeballs like sewing needles stabbed in a pin cushion.

"Why the heck am I so tired? Why am I only wearing a long-shirt, underwear, and socks? What the absolute f*ck is going on?"

And bam—I am out of it—*again.*

The next thing I remember is waking up, or semi-waking up, for the perceived second time with a bunch of girls staring at me.

No smiles. No chatter. Just blank faces frozen in an awkward silence.

Their eyes were glued to me like I was some arcane creature, whom they weren't sure whether to poke with a stick or report to the authorities.

"Where are we?" I managed to croak out to the curious bunch seated across from me.

You could hear a fish sneeze they were so quiet.

It was 'Lily' who let the air back into the room by asking how I was feeling, then led me to the kitchen for a glass of water. The others snapped their heads back to the telly, as if my actuality had sucked the life out of them like a leech latching on to its prey, siphoning their blood, their life, out of them.

"How long have I been here?" My voice shaky with confusion.

"About four days," she said matter-of-factly while I stood there in disbelief—where had my mind been this whole time?

Everything around me disappeared as my eyes drifted to the lush property, as I mulled over whether I really went that many days without eating or drinking anything.

Then... it-hit-me. I could not believe it. At fourteen years old, I had the bold nerve to run away from home and made the doomful decision to straight up vanish without a trace.

These impulsive missteps slammed into my mental machinery—comparable to the legendary power of linebacker Ray Lewis—who wrapped up his targets like steel cables, driving them into the ground as if they were as heavy as a pillow.

"What in the world did I get myself into?" I scolded to myself, unable to bear witness to this home-grown, pesticide-ridden pickle.

Mom wasn't about to sit around and wait for the Coppers to do their job. Nope. She went all out and hired a bounty hunter. A legit, world-traveling 'People Pursuer' who tracked fugitives for a living—to find me.

Around 1998 is when this extradition expert came with a guarantee that I would be found within three days.

And found... *I was.*

He caught me strolling down a busy street, casually puffing on a cigarette, thoroughly enjoying my chemically induced trance—

a smorgasbord of black-market scripts, cocaine, and alcohol that had been my steady diet over the last weeks.

As the Huntsman got close, he tackled me right there on the sidewalk. Laid me flat on my back before I could process what was going down. He immediately flipped me over, jammed his knee onto my sacrum, and cuffed me.

This Scoundrel Snatcher was not an itty-bitty man, mind you. Caught off guard, I found myself stunned beyond any line of rationalization.

There was zip I could say.

Staring blankly at the Collar Collector, I dug deep searching for any level of consciousness to work out what was taking place. This kind of element of surprise was a shocking doozy for me.

This Scallywag Snagger gave me his name in a tone that was calm yet commanding, as he explained he had power of attorney over me.

Immediately he dropped the hammer, *"There is nowhere for you to go. If you try to make a break for it, you will be thrown right into jail—not to the girls' home where we are headed now."*

I will say, fleeing him with cuffs on while my hands were locked behind my back was not a thought in my muddy mind. Truth be told, I had a weird sense of relief when he found me and that Mother saved me from this toxic trajectory.

The Cash-for-Capture Tracker gripped the cuffs tightly so he could guide me to his car. Destination: the airport. We were catching a flight—and yes—I was handcuffed on a plane.

How insane is that?

Thankfully, the cuffs were in the front by then—small wins.

At one point in the terminal, I began to feel humiliated once I noticed people staring at me. They must have been thinking, *"What did this girl do to put herself in this position?"*

All the stares from strangers burned into my skin like a magnifying glass on ants.

Either parents or adults whispered to kids as we waited to board. One can only assume they used me as their bad example teaching moment: *"See? This is what happens when you [little shits] don't listen."*

Glad to be of service.

Sarcasm and kidding aside, it's my hope that some part of this bundle of letters offers insight—or sparks a scintilla of inspiration.

On that note, my questionable life has always been the epitome of poor impulse control meets off-the-rails ambition—this will either be epic or court case material. Straight from the *"I shouldn't have survived that"* memory bank.

For the first time, I wanted to end that saga—erase it from my recollection forever, and start over living an idolized life.

Before waking up to the girls pointedly ignoring me on the couch—my last coherent memory of this entire debacle was the airport and getting on the first plane.

It took not one, but two separate planes. Two legs of whorligig travel to deliver me straight to Royal Hell—the high-risk girl's 'equestrian' boarding school nestled in Bend and Sisters, Oregon.

Add to that, I spent four days or more at the girls' home with no memories—and, well, astonished does not even begin to cover it.

After pounding a glass of water like I had stumbled out of the desert, dehydrated from an alcohol bender and sun poisoning, I was told to take a shower.

Once I was spic and span, they handed me another oversized shirt, socks, and underwear for the next rinse off—basically a moo-moo.

Truly the pinnacle of *"I have my shit together... nothing is going on here."*

Naturally, I asked Lily if I could borrow some pants and kicks because, you know, basic human dignity and all that fun stuff.

She calmly explained that I would be meeting someone named Steve soon to go over the rules, and at this stage of my initiation... pants, and shoes were apparently privileges I had yet to earn.

Fan-tabulous.

When I met with Steve at a dining room table, the first thing that came to mind was, *"Wow, look at this guy."* Not because we were almost the same height, but because he was broad with a stomach that seemed to enter the room a second before the rest of him.

It was clear from the get-go that Steve never missed a meal, and my immediate assumption was that I would be eating well.

Steve went in with the usual small talk, asking questions he already knew the answers to.

"Where are you from originally? What were you doing when the Bag-and-Tag Huntsman found you? Play any sports?"

Rustling within, I adhered to the casual etiquette, reluctantly obliging in the awkward pleasantries. Even so, Steve didn't delay before diving in—right where it *could* cut the deepest.

Without hesitation, he pried further into my background and dropped this gem, *"Have you ever been sexually abused or raped?"*

Sure, let me unload my trauma for you when I have no idea what has been going on in the last week, and you're a complete stranger.

Sincerely, I am fortunate to have never been molested. Rape is a blurred line, but those 'mishaps' did not take place until adult years.

One case in point: it started off as calm and consensual sex, only for his Cain-side to go ballistic during a drunken, blackout rage out of nowhere—violently hitting and choking me out. I pushed back frantically, but my arms were neither long enough, nor strong enough to stop his manhandle of...

He was now on a joyride.

Let's give credit to the maestro himself, *"Mr. Instrumentalist, did I miss anything? Yes?"*

Looks like Mr. Instrumentalist sold his house in Santa Cruz on 41st Avenue. He is possibly living his pipe dream in Costa Rica, groping through the unknown, while surfing and starring in his own *Hallmark* romance.

It tis' my hope this shout-out reaches him—unveiling his fake charm, musical inclination and full head of dark brown hair—all of it quite uncommon at our age.

Deplorably, these situations are far more common for women than most people come to terms with.

And here's the harsh truth: we rarely speak up. Not because our stories don't matter, but because the stigma is defeating, and the mere threat of revenge is brutal.

Enough of that winding, dark tunnel.

Steve erratically went over their never-ending rules because what's life without constantly dodging cracks in the pavement? Tiptoeing toward the smooth patches with every step just to avoid being cursed with misfortune.

He explained that my stay would be—in classically vague, cult-like-fashion, *"As long as you need to be here."*

Translation—until I turned eighteen. It all depended on my devotion, and if I was their little reliable worker bee who flawlessly obeyed every rule, kept my conversations to the exalted older girls ("OG"), and not a single word or gesture to the forbidden girls ("FG").

And, of course, worked tirelessly with no complaints, no backtalk, and without a lick of personality. This place was a straight-up nightmare.

Royal Hell ran on mind control and dominance—wielding threats, demanding amends through sacrifice, and stripping away whatever scraps of freedom they still allowed us to cling to.

Toilsome manual labor was on the docket nonstop, from dawn till they put a lid on the day.

To give you a taste of this domineering hierarchy, visualize this rehab and delirium exhibit with eight girls—only one was crowned as the OG ruling over the rest of us. She was the only one we were allowed to talk to while the rest of us were reduced to silent props in a perverted social experiment.

Need to use the restroom? Better hope everyone else does too, because if one girl had to go, all eight of us banded together like marching ants, following a trail of pheromones to carry a ply of toilet paperback to the colony.

Forget any gesture of humanity if you are an FG. No talking, no notes, no signals—no nothing.

It was like being trapped in a library where even your hippocampus firing, and sending electric impulses through your neurons felt too noisy. Where thinking itself, nerve rattlingly loud, could get you penalized.

Bumping into someone while eating or during manual labor?

Don't even contemplate apologizing. Sorry or having any eye contact with a FG was absolutely forbidden. Our only recourse was to muffle every orifice, keep our heads down, avert our eyes, whatever it took to camouflage the FG's as if they didn't exist.

We were a curious charade of coerced isolation, shoulder to shoulder with the very people we weren't allowed to acknowledge.

Step out of line, disregard a rule, and the corrections came swift: the infamous shit pile, a two-week wilderness boot camp, padded dark rooms with no windows, and if you hit that final strike—a call to the Rozzer to ship you off to ride the iron horse—orange jumpsuit season.

The most common punishment?

Shit pile, no joke.

This involved shoveling horse manure

into two buckets, hauling the pails a few yards, only to dump it out and repeat the process for what looked like all day.

Monotonous state of misery. Each bucket probably weighed just under fifteen pounds, give or take. It depended on how vintage the manure was.

Thankfully, I never had to partake, but I watched one *bad girl* carry it around with grim fascination. She was either there most days or sent off to the wilderness.

While we cleaned stalls for a few horses, most of the ponies roamed freely outside in the pasture, blissfully unaware of our shit show. However, there was one stall that was a nightmare unto itself—the stallion's.

Cleaning his stall was a sensory assault. You could not hold your breath long enough to finish the job, given that the stud had three separate droppings coming out of him.

The output was absolutely copious. It was so bad it could make you gag, or outright vomit on the spot. Honestly, I am not sure it was cleaned daily, which might explain the rank and rancid fumes.

Taking care of the horses did not bother me at first. We were told that once we were trusted, we would have the chance to ride. The simple thought of galloping, cantering, or barrel racing again had me transfixed.

I can only speak for myself, but at a certain point, the idea of riding horses took a back-seat to more basic needs. Like having enough food to eat, proper clothing and shoes, or even the luxury of talking to family on the phone.

No matter how backbreaking the labor, we were barely fed and hydrated given the intensity of our toiled slog-'n'-strain, dirty-duty grunt work.

Our days were spent sucking the life out of us beneath the sun—pulling weeds, wrenching up deep-rooted shrubs, mowing lawns, unloading hay and alfalfa bales by the truckload. Tackling whatever they threw at us.

Absolutely petrified of coming across as a whiny, little piglet—even if I was starving. Expressing any level of deprivation, had me frozen in fear of the inevitable payback and counterattack.

My chicken-hearted personality had my hocks knee-deep in pig manure. Kissing ass by working as hard as humanly possible. Clinging to the faint hope that—by some miracle—I might be rewarded with random feed, or even better, the ultimate prize, which was a trip into town with Steve and the swanky lot to eat actual restaurant food.

Steve would bring home extra fast food or leftovers, tossing them to us like scraps for malnourished stray dogs. All while we slaved away maintaining his sprawling acres.

He never actually stopped the car, though—it was a slow-creeper, food-by.

Almost like a gansta' hit drive-by, but with greasy edibles hurled into our gnawing hands before he sped off, leaving a cloud of dirt in his wake.

I vividly remember lunging forward once to catch a bag before it hit the manure-rich ground. Steve—ever the charmer—leaned out of his driver's window chuckling at my effort with his mini-Chiclet, gum-like teeth on full display.

How sad is it that I felt special for scoring their cast-off odds and ends? Pure freak-show entertainment at their disposal, wearing my desperation like a pantomime.

After an eternity, I earned the ultimate luxury: shoes and pants.

There is no way for me to overstate my elation at retiring from the hideous moo-moos. It's sanity-adjacent, how fast the basics start feeling bougie.

For most, having toe cages isn't a luxury, it's a necessity—like breathing—and without introspection, I took it for granted.

Almost like someone posturing as an overzealous partner who holds their 'better half' in the highest regard. When in reality, they're egotistical, self-absorbed, covert narcissists, and emotional vampires who conserve their effort and only *perform* socially when it benefits their ego.

Only to realize, out of nowhere, that these validation influencers with no content, no longer have someone by their side because their actions never matched the words... spewed out of their mouths.

Whoever was too ignorant with their fake persona, while valuing the unimportant things in life, is now left with the taxing remorse for undervaluing what they had.

Sole-savers blend into the backdrop of the daily grind until they're nowhere to be found. That's when the script-of-life changes hands during the plot-twist for another newly created bombshell.

Then suddenly, every pebble on the ground feels like a personal attack.

Wild, isn't it? How the basics only sparkle when they're dangled just out of reach?

Life was a different ball game back at my base camp. Mom's parents had a summer house in Clear Lake. We went to professional sporting events, theme parks, concerts—you name it. I was living the high-life without even realizing it, blissfully unaware of how marvelous I had it.

The Old Man was known as 'Kamikaze Ken.' He took us camping at the Delta in his twenty-five foot yellow day cruiser, aptly named Yellow-Fever. It was a boat that screamed midlife crisis and questionable judgment, a theme that ran strong in these outings.

I was part of a select club of underage kids allowed to hang out at Lost Isle, which was a 21-and-over hot spot in the 80s-90s, located in Stockton, California.

From photos, I guess that I was seven years old, standing on a stage with a live band, shaking a tambourine. The packed outdoor bar was wild with adults getting straight-up wasted, laughing, cheering, and having an exciting time.

Everything wasn't a conga line of good

times, though. I also witnessed my share of unsightly events. For instance, I saw more than one person tumble off the back of a boat into the water when it was shifted into gear.

Boating flubs weren't exactly rare, but one day was carved into my head-ham for all the wrong reasons.

A woman stood on the backrest at the rear of her boyfriend's boat. When he put it into gear, she plopped into the water behind the propellers. In a panic, he shifted into reverse to reach his damsel—only to run over his fräulein, severing one of her legs—clean—*off*.

Frozen in place, just a couple of feet away, I watched Dad's friend react instantly as he tried to shield the gore by covering my eyes and ushering me away—but it was too late. The image had already burned itself into my skull sponge.

Any-whoo...

On a far less traumatizing note, anything materialistic I wanted as a kid, was handed to me without a shiver of doubt. Not once was I disappointed for not receiving what I thirsted for.

A major fringe benefit of my parents' divorce? Their competitive spoiling wars. Each visit was a battle to one-up the other forebear's generosity—the upshot?

I got whatever my greedy-little-ego pleaded for, at that trending moment of time.

Reverting to the bad-girls' camp where all these realizations harrowed me sharply with remorse—like stepping barefoot on thumb tacks.

As quickly as those fleeting gut punches of clarity thoughts arrived, they withdrew just as swiftly.

The distance Royal Hell put between my family and I gave them ample time to work their brainwashing magic.

However, convincing me to do or say anything at that point in my life was not the erudite equivalent of effectively running the United States.

☠ DISCLAIMER ☠

The upcoming snazzy string-of-words is for entertainment only—purely my opinion, dipped in a creative conspiracy theorist point of view, with a healthy dose of *'just-for-fun.'*

Every word in this wee-book is protected under our First Amendment right to freedom of speech—covering political commentary, criminal government corruption, corporate lobbying, abuse of power, double standards, exposing misuse of federal authorities through gag orders on the private sector, self-publication of ideas, lived experience, information, parody, and satire.

Nothing here should be taken as counsel, advice, or endorsement. Unriddle these lines however you choose—I claim no burden on cognitive translations or afterthoughts that are engendered.

Let's be real, I am no brainiac. Just another 'Skool of Hard Knocks' graduate, clawing her way toward a street doctorate in Shit-Talking and Survival Studies.

Lights on, masks off:

It's almost like our world is so dirty that if everyone guilty of serious crimes were subject to disciplinary measures and sent to prison, we would only be left with a handful of people, and a lot of empty chairs at the table.

And isn't it ironic that JB's crew signed 8,064 pardons in four years? You just gotta ask—were they all signed with autopen?

This world is nothing more than a den of slithering snakes, pulling the strings while parading masked doubles to play everyone's part—we will never know who's actually who—hello, Central Casting!

There is no red—nor blue—only theatre for the world to view.

Every road coils back to the Viper's head. You know, those Reptilian Lords who have always served as the world's private banking cartels, and then some—who are blood-fed on human shed.

The Fed-with-no-Reserve is the serpent's crown, portrayed as a government entity. Only it's another scale in their world-rigging, malefic flank—as the Deep State kneels and society drowns.

The Roman Empire secretly rebranded, and expanded for the Boss-of-Tons— V a t t a - C u n t s . While Pope France-isss probed in robes, swallowing each soul to meet Satan's goal.

Hollyweird's elite make it rain by feeding off the human food chain—excuse me... with Barre-Klay, you say?

The See-Eye-A keeps hands in all— force-feeding the world eight balls for the Cabal.

Non-profit scum use 'God's House' as their smoke-and-mirrors to bleed His flock for their adreno-plus—so let's call their bluff and raise a fuss. Flaunting their corruption etched 'we protect innocents'—as they parade around with their blood-money pedigrees that fuel the Red Shoe Club.

Tech Lords with their joint-action entwinement for those who know—chant 3-3-3 incantations for the world show. Marrows drain, net-worths flare, all beneath the moon's iconic stare.

On 9-11-1990, G-H-W-B's new-world order was declared—with junior activating to increase their profit share—inflicting internal despair through God's eternal prayer.

Roth-childz, Rok-fellaz, the Boulé bunch, all sip from Ah-Loom-eh-Naughty's punch.

Du-Paunts, Moore-gans and War-bergs strobe the globe—filling up the Bushies who hum-hymns in-skinz on limbs, with their string of sins—Waltz-ing through vaults as the world defaults.

Fwee-Mae-sonz are the narrative surgeons who are writing the script as the Harry-mans steer the ships.

Blaqk-Rahk, Vanne-Garrd and the State-of-Streets—diverse racketeers of the modern age, torching down towns—backstage.

Could it be—Ha-Why-E... you see?

Or maybe—L.A.—the play repeats today.

Royal Crownie and Orsin-ee heirs, laying ground rules for billionaires:

Suckie-Zuckie-B, Pokie-Gatez, Bozo-Bezo, Chat-Alt-Man, Sore-ohs, Buff-ette—all shake beneath one velvet tree, sacrificing you and me—trading our currency for towers of gold, for a world that is oversold, eightfold.

Fedz feast on their offspring—military intelligence handed over to the private sector to spy—f*cking over laws while the authorities stand by—maxing out bribed-up defiance, straight into staged compliance.

Flipping the bird with patriotic avoidance, slurring the Constitution as they toilet-bowl its importance.

It's a rogue gallery of greed where the grift runs high. An endless cycle of dirty deals drifting by—the shadow-slick funds, f*ck the truth with lie after lie.

We don't vote for them, yet they vote to lock us out by the trillions. They lecture capitalism—but on the sly, it's a secret coup.

Tons of names, but only one echo scripting our silence.

They own the 'book of life.' Our pages pre-written while we dance blindfolded on their world stage.

Vultures in silk ties, fluent in lies—manipulating markets, bulk-buying our futures. These Vipers prepay and pad their insurance to save their bottom-line—from the fallout of disasters, contrivedly wrought by design. Set-in-motion during their secret-society club sessions, by invitation only for the 'World's String-Pullers.'

Intermediaries around their finger—corporate and government alike—stay under their thumb, steering us numb.

Endless contracts owned through black-mail plots, quietly smoking us out as they reshape our thoughts—our structures, our soul routes—we're disfigured-and-drained to reduce our 'playtime' as they fuel their next gain.

We are pieces placed on a board they

configured—a Global game where we are disfigured. Forced to our knees to be at their beck-and-call—we are silenced within our own downfall.

Surprise, surprise—corruption you can't sanitize.

D-Oh-D and the Pent-Ah-Gone, selling blockbuster propaganda since 1927. Manufacturing myths as a polished weapon, Arm-Ah-Geddin. Predictive programing masked as a prophecy from Heaven.

Ridiculous slush-fund budgets for back-door deals, only to steal—Ah-Murica's meals.

In the last five years our *'honorable'*—the keepers of truth, the whole truth, and nothing but the truth—has burned through at least 5.25 trillion dollars on black-box tech, surveillance toys, and shadow-state instrumentation.

With that kind of damned allocation, there should be no perv, pedo, trafficker or drug smugglin' Cartel, prowlin' any Ah-Murican' location.

See-Eye-A, Eff-B-Eye, Bureaucrat or not—
no one earns a sick salvation—weed these
f*ckers out with ruthless dedication.

How does the See-Pee-S—ah, forgive the
slip—how does an essential component for
child trafficking evade justice... every time?

Our shot-colla's and 'communities' stand
tall for the Mo-saud—every tool, every trick,
they permit—reverse split. When did we
become Izz-railz bait and switch?

To those who pretend to protect the
American people, but turn around and
make decisions by listening to the rustle of
your own pockets being lined—yes-you,
penis whistlers—you have earned some new
ceremonial titles:

Bureau of Constitutional Desecrators.
Govies Who Strip Americans of Freedom.
Official Liars, Thieves & Murderers.

While big Farm-ah plays its barter game
beneath the public's eyes, trading health for
wealth—pure quid-pro-quo disguised as
life-saving therapies.

Ahem, WHO?

Fow-Chi!

W.E.T.S.[3] not miss our insider-trading traitors, saboteurs, and defector politicians... do-they-all-wear-every-title?

What up Pill-Oh-See? Bye-Dumb? Ohh-Bomb-Ah? BIG Mike?

And, of course, the glue to the crew: Mr. and Mrs. Killers—oops, I mean Klinn-Tonz. Their body count amounts to over sixty headcounts, give or take a few. They will never make it through—the ones who see, who-know-too-much—you see, blows come to thee.

All handled *neatly* by the Eff-B-Eye or See-Eye-A—any contractor that will take the hits—anesthetize heart attacks—SAC 46.

X-See-Eye-A—*"We kill people based on metadata."* -2014

Err'body that has ever been in big Whities House, fiddle-faddle the world of these coincidences, look at our innocence. Don't mind their construction—nah, it ain't nothin' new. *East-Side* sponsors diggin' deeper underground tunnels, too. Funnelin' them Lizzies 'n' kidz, truth be told—they are paving the underworld in blood and gold.

Kholburt's show is in its final season—is he bowin' out, or is there a wild reason? He chased his dream guest, the big one he hoped—the dick swingin' Pope.

Kholburt be singing songs while makin' dem kids dance, only to scare them in a trance. Painting their faces to portray the lie, high on crystal meth—they make them die.

Goblets full of blood—throttle through the club—first-hand grubs on that pineal gland *drug.*

Sign-Fell'd literally said fresh-flesh tastes like a 'spongy pancake,' the kind that trembles on the plate with every breath you take.

The Eff-B-Eye buried Weenie's laptop, buh-bye—tucked it in a vault so deep even roaches can't pry. And no matter how they spin-it, they be in-it—won't stop at nuttin'—to win-it.

Private jets, war debts—Whall Stweet pets.

Make some noise for Gee-Dub-Ya—the Skull-'n'-Bones—Old Yail-er.

Flaunting thirty-three degrees as a Fwee-Mae-son—See-Eye-A-Puppet, turned certified traitorz.

Toss in J-Carrie—stir in Schwartzies lot. Blaqk-Stowne, Blaqk-Rahk, same throne, same plot.

They all preach with their blood-money gospel, carved-in-innocents and buried-by-rocks.

15 new seniors, their rituals are clear—they pass the torch—every Yail-year.

Reset the world-stage, rehearse the lie—while we sit back—forced to absorb their lies—*dry*.

W.E.T.S.[3]

World. Endorsed. Tyranny. System.
Wealthy-Elites Tapping-Systems.
Whistleblowers—Erased
Truth—Suppressed.

Thousands of loyal lemmings, hidden in plain sight, clinging to the Vipers' inside-out pockets. Materially incentivized, integrity evicted, would be legally convicted but those in power omitted—they're committed to the See-Eye-A's blackmail for that crack sell, not to end up on their blood-trail.

Meanwhile, us tax-paying citizens claw it it out in the fictitious *Land of the Free.* We are forced into their hunger-n-robbed games in the District of 50 States—as our *intelligence* snuffs out anyone who speaks out.

The Hollyweird Elite rake in government subsidized insurance for their multi-million-dollar mansions, while we are being swindled and defrauded on every penny that is over-taxed.

Maybe it's over my dullard-head, but I sure do admire that Magna Carta, we sure otta like it's 1215—back when they only eased up once somebody seized the King's purse.

One special-ed policymaker, the *Highness* of C-State's fate—funnels-fire-funds, through nonprofits' gate. The Queen of his world, all shimmer and pearls—breeding the homeless, defrauding the hopeless—his charity dressed as a decoy.

His pockets rapidly expand as families die, fanning their embers with polished lies. Sipping *French* red as the smoke drifts high, his money washed in the *Laundry*'s eye.

These 'Executives and Agencies' squander our money, then devastate us with false-flag catastrophes—distracting us with preplanned tragedies—offering brief disclosures for those reading in-between the lines, while keeping all powerless in their unethical stranglehold.

OPERATION NORTHWOODS...

On September 10, 2001 Rumsfeld let it be known: $2.3 trillion dollars in transactions, blown. Nothing but charades, ledgers never obtained—I would rot in a cell for a decade if I played that way.

The Patriot Act grants illegal loopholes, through muzzle 'n' mute controls—usurping our Amendments: constitutional ruptures of a fatal degree, for you and me—stress fractures of every stature—while Tech and financial institutions hand over 'dog door,' *compelled-compliance*—fraudulent alliance.

They all-be spying—micromanaging taxpayers $600 transfers, forcing citizens to prove our innocence—yet the govies waste hundreds of trillions of our honest pay, with no delay, as they diligently ensure consequences will never come their way.

Whore-With-No-Wits has nuttin' to show in 13 years—not even Fine... fined. They both toe'd the lines, echoing systemic violations, only to sanction blanket immunities as they misuse their authorities. Albeit predictably, brazenly, and on the daily, you see, it's their unwritten... PAH-Luh-See.

Inspector G's job description based on zero referrals—ever—to the DOJ for FISA abuse: *"Simulate accountability through carefully worded reports. Never refer our systemic misconduct beyond administrative theater—stay clean on paper by updating the public that policies were revised and new training was implemented.*

Remind the agents and contractors that intelligence privileges are to be exploited quietly, personal gain is obviously acceptable, but discretion is our priority. Laws exist only for the public. Even when we get caught, we will never face the consequences—that said, use your senses and erase your disgraces.

So much deception to pacify Americans—when does it end? What about obligations to protect this Nation through indictments and litigation?

Federal laws apply to all dirty rats, govie or not—President Trump, I must confess this is a holy mess, are you having any success?

Our hard-earned cash is literally missin' every year—the Pent-Ah-Gone refuses to comply—it is utterly unclear. When will it be a crime to waste all of our dimes, as the Viper's stand by to receive their bottom-line.

No investigations, while costs go up with that runaway inflation.

Burning our wages, our funds dissipatin', in the last twenty-five years, $45.2 trillion dollars straight-up evaporatin'—between all the green lines—it's a conservative number by design.

As generations die, the truth decays—none remember the Sixteenth for the fraud it became. The Founders etched a creed of limits: small government bound with the people unbound. Taxation was meant to be a passing storm, not iron chains binding a nation—scuffing us toward starvation and early cremation.

Let us not forget the See-Eye-A's *ventures* with Eye-Que-Tee—a pivotal, mostly digital investment with our *pennies*. Are they dishing out all that *seed* money as 501(c)(3)? Real funny. The CEO's last check? About $5 millie. Will it ever end—and what about our dividends?

Of course PAL-in-Tier is in the mix, is it always a fix? Gripping tight on that $10 billie govie contract—is their paper trail of monies in tact?

In the interim, some are making it rain for their human-trafficking buddies, and money laundering *fweinds,* all for the benefit of our dirty-ass, so-called—elite.

We always have money for the ~175 out of 195 countries in the world that we support and fund, but never U.S. citizens as 'they' snicker-in-amusement-and-greed, fully-convinced-we-will-'*never*'... **WAKE-UP-AND-STAND-UNITED.**

Realize en masse how these f*ckers are running our country into the ground as the dirties hit us with friendly-fire—because yes, the See-Eye-A lives and works... by *our* side.

End of my viewpoint-based, *comical* rant. The preceding text constitutes personal conjecture, parody, and satirical commentary intended solely for entertainment and creative exploration. It contains no verified facts, no accusations, nor representations.

Any resemblance to real persons—alive or dead—entities, or situations is coincidental, exaggerated, or simply the fault of the internetz. This was explicitly intended for humor and thee archaic... writing boundaries.

And let's be real, I don't have the clearance or connections to corroborate anything—this is merely a creative-jest that I like to call my 'String-Puller Theory.'

Burden-of-proof? **POOF** ↻

Back to the high-risk girl's home, shall we?

It took months before I was allowed to talk to my family over the phone. Sure, we wrote letters, but every-single-word had to be supervised.

The reasons behind the lack of regular communication were conveniently withheld. Leaving me blind to the manipulative web they were spinning that my family didn't really care. If they did, why wasn't I home with them instead of being shipped off to exist elsewhere?

The planted idea that my family didn't see me as a priority, moldered within.

When the big moment came, I was allowed

to speak to my family. 'Sue,' Steve's partner or significant other, was stationed beside me to to make sure I followed the script. She would rehearse each line with me beforehand, then hovered over my shoulder like a drill sergeant, ensuring every word I babbled passed the Royal Hell inspection.

I dutifully recited the lines: *"I am so happy to be here! Work on the property is keeping me active. We are fed well, and I am not ready to leave yet because I can already see the positive impact this place is having on me."*

Side note: laziness was never an issue in my humble-means family.

When the family eventually visited, I was wavering in diplomacy—conflicted between the two. Instinctively, I tried to be loyal to both sides, never once weighing my needs. Torn between what they drilled into me at Royal Hell, and what my heart knew to be true.

Given that I was—let's face it—mentally defective, Sue and Steve had no trouble exploiting me. 143

They were...

**Sleezy - Breezy,
Morally Loose ...
Money Squeezy.**

My life dangled at their fingertips. I would have said or done anything they instructed. When you really think about it, I wasn't just another troubled girl to them—I was their meal ticket, we all were.

Make no mistake, they were not ingenious masterminds. Far from it. What they had instead was an edge—the advantage of life experience.

They had years to refine their skills in profiteering and deceitful exploitation, enough to make them look like experts to a group of vulnerable, impressionable girls. Not geniuses—seasoned con artists who knew how to work the system and us.

Family trusted Steve and Sue, but they questioned their tactics. Opa, my mother's father, flew in unannounced. Sadly, he was granted only ten minutes with me before being shown the door.

Either way, Royal Hell robbed the naïve for personal gain, using mind control to seal the deal. Their off-brand, contorted reasoning, locked air-headed tight in my inner sanctum.

A couple of the girls on my level—and all the OGs—seemed to have rare, sought after permissions. Meanwhile, I was left to speculate why I wasn't favored at all, since I worked my fingers to the bone with every joyous task they threw my way.

Terrified of even the smallest mistake, I pushed myself to the absolute limit to be unquestionably on top of it all. The textbook definition of a notable kiss-ass—all to dodge the nightmares they dangled over our heads.

Not by stars, nor the heavens above was I receptive to being sent to the wilderness program after hearing the horror stories about it. The idea of shit pile sucked, but it was the only sanction mechanism that was remotely doable.

As for the dark room with no windows? I would not have survived that mentally.

Even though I have yet to encounter an integrity driven, non-corrupt police officer, or government peacekeeping agent, I wasn't exactly in a rush to test the waters by breaking the rules.

To dispel the shade I am casting over the Blue Line, let me say this: I fully support and respect law enforcement—the good ones, anyway. I don't want the fiasco you are about to read overshadow my guileless sentiment.

I am—will always be—a true patriot who deeply respects honorable officers. To those who serve with a fortress of virtue, my gratitude runs deep.

After a few months, I was endorsed to attend high school with the other girls. Of course, the same ridiculous rules applied.

Talking to anyone other than the OGs?

Not happening, mostly. If I needed to speak to a teacher, it was strictly schoolwork related only. Small talk, witticism, or—perish the thought—any actual human interaction with non-OGs was off-limits.

Seeking out a counselor—or anyone, for that matter—was full-stop, off the table. If shit hit the fan, we were to find an OG, brief them, and they would pass it along to Steve or Sue before the school staff.

Avoiding conversations with kids in the hormone-fueled halls was easy enough, given the strict boundaries placed on us. I quickly jumped the gossip line as the whispered about 'new girl,' added to the collection of at-risk teens. Curiosity swirled, but no one was tempted to cross the invisible line to talk to me.

This here lump-of-logic was unbothered by the stares and gossiping. Socializing or making friends was nowhere on my radar. Not only did I need space to process it all, the last thing I wanted to do was make an already precarious situation worse.

Serendipitous timing placed me in the school's creative writing class—my first brush with poetic expression, a doorway to cathartic purge and the faintest shimmer of hope on Royal Hell's horizon.

At fifteen, I wrote my first poem. Back then it was titled, 'Hurt.' Today it lives on as, 'The Pain I Felt Inside.'

Fast-forwarding to about a year into Royal Hell, I was called into the main house and informed that the home was shutting down. My family was already on the road, driving from California to Oregon to pick me up.

This news overwhelmed me with joy— I practically vibrated with excitement. The OG's had their skepticism and reminded me that I was not yet equipped to mingle with the party influencers. Grand assurances were given to the OGs that I would be forthright.

To my complete disadvantage, all the OG's wisdom went in one ear and right out the other. Nothing mattered except for being a free bird, again.

With self-reliance blazing into view, I sprinted to our sleeping quarters roosted above a massive barn to chat with the girls I had never been allowed to speak to before, now that the ball was back in my court.

Cancerian pinch from my defiant claws.

Thoroughly foolish and riding high on misplaced confidence, I was half-asked sure that I was ready to be a model student. Purely optimistic that there were no trickster maneuvers in the back of my processing plant.

When I returned to my hometown in Cali, I tried me damnedest to persuade myself that my shot-calla' needed to be the white-light Heavenly Angel, serenely poised on my right side.

But then, a tickle crept up the left side of my neck—the whisper of the Fallen Angel's tongue—thirstily inclined to provoke the promised land of reasoning.

The Beast's darkness began to slither closer its subtle, seductive hiss. This was a sly reminder to my subconscious that deals were ready to be made. The Caspian cobra sank its fangs into my jugular, more than ready to release its venom if I refused what my vain heart was offered.

All I needed to do was ask, and I shall receive. A life filled with double-fisted pleasures full of idle indulgences, all under the Prince of Darkness' watch.

Temptation was ready to play its hand.

Home for donkey's years, I had plenty of stomping grounds to frequent, especially now that I was of legal age to drown all my life-dependent organs in liquor without begging anyone to buy it for me.

Social media was out. One night, in my usual lubed-up-haze, a notification slid across the screen—a private group had added me to their chat. Lo and behold, it was a group message from the Royal Hell girls, and others I never met before.

This was during my most harrowing of blackout days—around 2007—when my pain ran as deep as the Mariana Trench. Squeaked by as the queen of drowning my sorrows as I performed the heaviest of chemical miracles. In tandem, I misdirected those around me so they would conclude that I was thriving with a good head on my shoulders.

One OG had an irresistibly positive and happy spirit—incomparable soul to anyone I have met before, passed away. The news was both grievous and jarring—hitting me like Spider Silva's elbow to the cavity of my chest.

It breaks my heart to this day the people we lose due to unresolved traumas.

♥ C.M. Rest in Peace. You Are Missed. ♥

As time went on in the chat, the mood began to shift. The soul-crippling remarks about Royal Hell left me stunned beyond belief.

Without hesitation, I jumped online desperate to find out what had gone on at Royal Hell and who was involved—striking myself with rapid relief and an unsettling craze. I was slightly consoled by the fact that I had never been granted any special privileges.

At the same time, I was outraged, and nauseated to learn the sexual horrors that unfolded while I was there.

Steve and Sue initially alleged they closed Royal Hell out of concern for a boy they wanted to adopt. A child who they said, *"Shouldn't grow up around at-risk girls."*

This boy was the son of one of the OGs, just a toddler then, maybe two years old when I was there.

The kind of revelation that left me reeling, scowling in the layers of deception and the dawning realization of what had been hidden all along.

It appears that a few brave girls came forward with their traumas in or around late 1999, prompting officials to investigate the callous acts committed against young girls.

Criminal Mistreatment. Sexual Abuse. Money Laundering. And—then—some.

Back then, the Oregon Police walked their talk with their tagline, *'To Protect and Serve,'* which was not victim catnip—they meant it.

In stark contrast, the conscience-shocking betrayals by the Monterey Police Department ("MPD") in California, have their own way of selective enforcement.

Based on my direct experience... the MPD thrives in mendacity while portraying themselves as the public-safety guardians, only to convert into conspirators behind closed doors. Shielding the crimes of the Viper's tail while trampling state and federal laws alike.

All to preserve the Pelican's gilded seats of power, embedded deep within the government and private sector.

My scars remain the evidence, now that it's clear the Pelican's *institutions* are both the butchers and liars. The hands that carved my heart from my chest, and the mouth that swore no harm was ever done—no blood was shed. As they profane the oath once sworn to uphold.

MPD's motto might boast about truth and

integrity—but let's be real—it's all buzz-bait.

With my ever-so-generous opinion, and funny spirit, I decided to lend a sharp hint of satire-and-parody hand for the MPD's marketing department, by crafting a tagline that truly echoes their operations with *me*.

Let's manage expectations for when I am in town, shall we?

"Responsive to the corrupt.

Second to those [Monique] who do not have their interests aligned with us—the dirty Pigs and the elite power we serve for those monetary favors that keep our banks rollin.'

Every time since money and power are the true shot-callin' kings.

Holla for that dolla!"

If only the MPD had taken a page from the Oregon officers' handbook. Perhaps then they might have taken my life-threatening complaints seriously. Instead, they chose to flagrantly neglect their duties.

Alas, their 'public service' was a ritual of

erasure—truth orphaned, evidence ghosted, silence weaponized. They wore apathy like armor and called cowardice their procedure.

I will always keep the faith that there are still those with moral soundness. People who intrinsically hold themselves accountable. That no matter what or who, they will always honor the oath because they swore to protect the vulnerable and serve their communities with unwavering integrity.

To those Oregon Detectives, I commend you. You didn't resort to a condescending—gas-lit silver-tongued—deception.

Nor did you parade around as if you treat women with a *second-to-none,* virtuous stance while pulling unethical stunts behind closed doors.

Now, for the flagrantly unconstitutional spectacle. This is an unfiltered take on my run-in with their soul-snatcher 'manual', penned by Pelican's Tellin' Porkies for the Grifters of Monterey. That unpublished, unofficial, backroom guide to principled bankruptcy.

These Hell-Bound Hustlers whispered doctrine of deceit seems to dictate as follows:

"It is the opposite day for California and Federal laws when dealing with Monique.

Why? Well, we made a pact with the dirty-ass elite hands that we shamelessly kiss. We simply can't resist since we move to the pull of our DNA—the only way we know.

We must annihilate her life—either she goes down, or we do.

Monique is sharper than the credence we gave her—and she's got the guts to back it up. She called us out face-to-face and refused to let this go. She's ethically driven, values her life, and most importantly, she needs only one person willing to fight for her rights—someone with ironclad ethics and the authority, the moral backbone to take us down.

We can't go to prison—do you have any idea what they will do to us?

By all means, let's turn her life into a Pelican Brief conspiracy sequel. After all, our appetite for corruption will never be exposed.

We'll keep thriving on collusion and atrocious greed. Filing our insolence receipts to be paid on the taxpayers' dime, while promotions and hush money from the de facto shadow authorities keep elevating us... *up-the-chain.*

We hereby pledge our most effective weapon: redact the record and rewrite the narrative—quietly resolving every electronic embarrassment and incriminating file.

These unethical avenues are merely a perk—an amuse bouche to keep our skills sharp—ensuring those with the true string puller power deem us worthy, and anoint us for the next ascent.

We all agreed if Monique sees a red sniper light on her chest while comfortable inside her home—sipping coffee—that will for sure push her over the edge. Executed brilliantly by the way—the red dot sight locked right onto her heart.

Monique caught its reflection in the window, then confirmed the tactical sight when she looked down.

Although we never anticipated that she would say the name of the person she thought targeted her on camera during our house call later that day. We sort of panicked, bolting out of there so fast we sounded like we nearly tumbled down her stairs.

We must be careful, Monique does not hold back one bit. Another on the record faux-pas would be risqué, even for us. It's too dangerous to keep scrubbing the record.

I busted my gut so hard saying *"It's too dangerous,"* that my micro, baby-carrot-peen made me pee myself. Ah, so warm—the only wetness I can get.

But wait... a quick update for the new Pelican-lemmings that just joined in the fun.

WIMPP-MPSLAW has been instructed to evade her calls asking for the fake U.S. Marshal's identity—because, well, it's him.

All of her *"Please-help-save-me pleas"* will never get investigated since our head Pelican is a major player in town. Who am I kidding, we also have the FBI and other intelligence 'authorities' who have our backside.

No question we denied the Pelican names she gave on camera to CBK-FHOA and OTH.

Stealing evidence while impersonating a Federal Marshal?

Of course—we've mastered that move.

Fraudulently removing anything we want, thanks to our government-hacker connections and unchecked power?

You betcha! After all, who's going to stop us?

No one has the nerve to go against their own. And, with so many of us involved, our combined connections will shut it down before it even gets off the ground.

It will take Monique years to recover. If she ever does, given what we have done. We scared her out of California and left her life in shambled ruins, with her fragile family torn apart in the crossfire.

In addition, in or around February 2024, Monique purchased a new phone and changed her number so we used this email: PeterChabot2015@ ... to install a local host so we don't keep using government gear to monitor her.

We are back in the game Person Ones!"

And... Scene.

So, what are my acronyms?

For the record, I concealed identities since I take privacy seriously—no flibbertigibbet here. *"I-would-never"* want to damage them fake reputations.

CBK-FHOA: Corrupt Bobby Kast, F*cks His Own Ass—yep, by poking his thumb up his butt.

What, what? In the butt. (Samwell song)

While in the interview room, live on their camera, I spoke to CBK-FHOA and OTH—named Bous-ted and Schur-er who is the head Pelican—I even handed him Schur-er's physical address.

CBK-FHOA only asked for Mom's phone number to substantiate my allegations—yet, he never called. Ultimately, the green camera light activating on Mum's phone while she wasn't using it—along with her location being spoofed to Cedar Mill, Oregon—indicated she had been hacked.

Meanwhile, OTH—Officer Tater Head—was looking for his brain to pop back into place. But, it was too small to find, and as time passed, he forgot what he was doing.

OTH's, dimwit-nitwit, half-wit brain, remained scattered everywhere. Not that it matters—he is living proof that intelligence comes in fractions, and even with all three—he still isn't playing with a full deck.

Now for the grand finale, we have—'Detective' WIMPP-MPSLAW.

Better known as: Where-Is-My-Pee-Pee? My-Pee-Sounds-Like-A-Woman!

Taking his performance to Oscar-worthy levels, WIMPP-MPSLAW impersonated a Federal agent while in plain clothes and bullet proof vest with no insignia.

When I asked him for his Marshal badge or any type of credential on three separate occasions, he kept flicking me from his conscience.

WIMPP-MPSLAW adamantly lied while on the clock as a Monterey detective that he worked in the San Jose U.S. Marshal's office, promising to get all the fatal cyberstalking, and death threats into the hands of the federal authorities.

WIMPP-MPSLAW gave me supreme comfort and confidence when he said:

"You're in good hands now. This will be investigated, this is why we have federal courts. Where is all your evidence?"

I told him where my contemporaneous notes and SD cards were located—real-time videos of intercepted calls with deaths threats captured through a Bluetooth free

Cybershot which lived beyond the Pelican's hacking reach, and undeveloped disposable cameras. Most critically, 'objects' were preserved to test for traces of poison.

Then, as if slipping into a casual gossip session, WIMPP-MPSLAW said the head Pelican's company—or perhaps the P.O.S. himself, was under investigation.

"For what?" I asked. *"Was it tax evasion or something?"*

Silence. No response.

There were at least three other Monterey Police Officers who stood by for this grand show. The one woman was decked out in SWAT-like gear when she barreled toward me like I was a f*king terrorist—striking me with a riot shield and twisting my wrists with unreasonable force—ludicrously concerning.

The officer who stood by the studio was the only one I thought might tell the truth about WIMPP-MPSLAW's patent lies. I met him *personally* when I was fifteen years old— later on he portrayed himself as ethical now that he had a son... Do as I say, not as I do?

But in reality, they were all in on it. So, yeah, maybe my optimism is just naïveté.

The MPD's real subterfuge methodology: divert all negative attention onto me. The so-called, *off-the-trolley* victim because these sorry-ass, Pelican Rogue Agents got caught with their pants down. Figuratively, thank the stars.

As a lower-class taxpayer, I have no civil rights because I was not—am not—dirty scum like them.

These honorable Oregon detectives, true to their vocation, sought justice for the girls at Royal Hell by refusing to bend-the-knee to white collared, deceit-dealers.

Nor did Oregon cave to social status, influence, and the undeniable connections to the puppets of greed—like how the Monterey rats wield countless leveraged resources in their back pocket.

There is a slight relief to know there are still truthful advocates out there. People who don't abuse their powerful authority or influence.

Instead, these Sisters or Bend detectives respected our civil rights, irrespective of who committed the vile act, any potential connections they may have had, or any pressures that could have been exerted by their commanding peers to look the other way.

Oregon's public safety avoiding such depravity at that time speaks volumes. It suggests that moral fiber exists in some places, even if it seems to be a rare commodity.

Now, fully back to Steve.

An indictment by a secret grand jury resulted in a staggering forty-five counts of criminal charges. The list included first and second-degree rape, penetration, abuse, criminal mistreatment, and so on.

Quotes from the Bulletin: *"I think you calculated and premeditated this scam from day one, Tiktin told Gage before the victims* and family in the courtroom. It took tremendous conceit and contempt to proceed with this plan of yours. The cruelest part was the isolation imposed on these girls and the disaffection you created between them and their families. You made them so dependent upon you for favors they would do anything you wanted."

"During Tuesday's hearing, prosecutors said Gage doled out privileges and gifts to the young women who gave in to his sexual advances. Those who did not were punished."

"Victims said Gage told them they did not matter to their parents. He threatened to send them to wilderness camps or have them locked up in mental institutions if they did not behave as he wished."

Steve was detained with a one-million-dollar bond. Sue initially had nine counts of criminal mistreatment—she skated away with no charges thanks to Steve pleading guilty—how convenient.

I vehemently disagree with Sue's outcome,

but Karma—unyielding as ever—always has a knack for evening the score.

I-am-all-for-it.

In its own time, Karma finds the most fitting way to balance the scales—often at the worst moment for the one due to spiritual alignment. At least, that has been my humbled yet thoroughly lived observation.

Shortly after Steve received his forty-five year prison sentence, he married Sue in a jailhouse ceremony.

Only to then... commit suicide.

Royal Hell managed to get away with their abuse of power for years, and I question how no one saw, or at least recognized, what was happening behind closed doors.

Hard for me to believe that not one outsider suspected anything. My memory might be a tad hazy, but I vaguely recall Steve having some sort of connection with Johnny Law or juvie, something along those lines.

Looks like Sue had some connection to Sister's small-town school board which was an unexpected detail.

Was she involved in local affairs to influence the school's narrative while also keeping a pulse on what outsiders thought? I ask because this statement only came out after the fact:

"The Sisters School District had a close and unusual relationship with Steve Gage, allowing him to bring his 'drug dog' to the high school without checking his background and making him a truancy officer. Gage's behavior was noted as belligerent and controlling, and he was allowed to roam the school hallways freely, which enabled him to spy on and control the girls' actions."

People in small, confined towns usually know all that 'good-gossip.' The fact that no one connected the dots—or chose not to—is as unsettling as the abuse itself, as the criminal mistreatment was patently clear.

From what I have gathered, Royal Hell

was not regulated like other boarding schools due to parents signing over guardianship. The laws might have been different, allowing them to bypass the need for any special licenses and oversight.

I stand firm in my belief that those who have transcended extreme hardships are uniquely equipped to offer guidance on how to lead others toward the truth of what inner cleansing entails.

When this insight is combined with the expertise of industry professionals, those with formal education but not necessarily high-level personal trauma—it would create a powerful dynamic.

An unshakable truth for me is that these mind-manipulating wounds require a collective effort to develop effective, well-rounded strategies for healing.

To safeguard this process, it's imperative to involve more than one psychologist or specialist, thereby reducing the risk of negligence and human error.

It is critical to limit the chance of fate twisting mistakes when someone seeks support for a suitable, therapeutic path.

Why gamble with a life by placing all responsibility on a single person?

As I embrace the future, I look forward to cultivating relationships that would allow me the honor of putting my hard-earned life contusions to beneficial use.

My hope is to empower individuals of any age that are facing adversity, where life hasn't worked out in the way they wished for.

Those who—exactly like me at various points in my life—desperately longed for the guidance, support and encouragement.

Sup' Psychologists? I Am... Damaged Goods!

Mental damage was inflicted by Dad who was damaged mentally. Commingling with an array of other emotional landmines, had me drowning in distilled distractions as I aimlessly wandered highways in numb unconsciousness—disjoined from owning my choices while lost in a maze of brain hiccups.

Others piled on as they added insult to injury whether knowingly or not. Somehow, I managed to stockpile the misery—stacking a tower-of-torment atop an already hyper reactive mental state—tripping me head first into a psychological *Mayday*.

At its core, my early life calamities laid the foundation for me to swallow my struggles as I turned away from cognitively induced challenges, and pretended that everything was gumdrops and jellybeans.

Now for the swift rundown, of my previously broken down... soup-for-brains. Here is the veritable checklist of brainwave bottlenecks:

Jealousy, auto-destructive patterns, and dire FOMO? Those were my first, middle, and last names.

Possessive and controlling tendencies? Of course, why wouldn't I cling to people like Gorilla Glue while holding myself hostage? Exerting uninvited help onto anyone else, to try and fix their all, *except* myself.

People-pleasing and codependency? My two-for-one special. I did it all for you while over-apologizing as if I were bleeding out ink for a Pulitzer Prize. Even as I bent over backward, I somehow still managed to say *"Thank you!"*

Fawning? I could have won doormat of the year with everyone—*every* year.

Hyper-critical? Oh, absolutely. No one is good enough, least of all... me.

Over-analyzing?

Why settle for one worst case scenario, when I can conjure up 10,000? Only to be dumbfounded by the one person I never saw coming.

Catastrophizing? Ah... can it be true that I have an uncanny knack for turning death threats into a one-way ticket to a looney-bin overload? Courtesy of a kangaroo-court arrest and the implosion of my entire life?

Wait, that literally happened: Monterey Police, Chief Hober, Mike Garcia, Richard Castellon, Jesse Phillips, Jake Pinkas, US Marshal Elliott, Trevor Zink, Dolores Leal, Gloria Allred, San Jose Internal Affairs and Rob Bonta... PLUS.

Let me try this again—every molehill mutates into Chimborazo?

Depression? There is nothing that beats a good hyperventilating cry while fearing for your life in the fetal position and entombed in the blankets. Add in catatonic living, see-saw diet and hygiene hiatus—peak self-care, am I right?

a disastrous self-image paired with Neurotic overthinking and some passive-Aggressive tendencies? add a sprinkle of Validation cravings, and i became Your recipe for "look at me, what do you Even think? please like me as i quietly re-Sent you for it—oh yeah... cute outfit too, Quisling."

Escapism? Oh, that's just me playing a never-ending game of *"Where's Mo?"* Except, I never once bothered to look for myself. A timeless tale of self-deception by hiding in the open while never honoring myself.

The inability to establish or enforce boundaries turned me into the world's most decorative, pushover-wuss. With my spooked-by-abandonment issues, deformed every text and casual *"See you later,"* into a Lion King rehash of Mufasa falling to his death.

My self-consciousness fueled by an inferiority complex and impostor syndrome, had me juggling chaos like an Olympic sport.

Except, I was more of a wannabe break dancer with laughable, amateur moves. Nothing like the jaw-dropping skills of the real pros in Red Bull competitions.

I overindulged in alcohol and substances as if they were my cardinal food groups—all because the mirror and I were never on speaking terms. Meanwhile, my hangover out bench pressed me into submission.

Didn't I sound like a winner?

Now, let's try to conceptualize this mental torment on repeat—interrogating myself through every interaction—while struggling to keep those darker reflexes and negative manners from spilling out, posing as if I were healthy and that my life was *perfect*.

All those Daddy issues along with other indefensible life incidents never harmed me at all—browbeating and flagellating myself by reminding me that I wasn't a pussy, so I'd better not act like one.

But, deep down—*deep down*—I knew. Instinctively I understood these negative impulses were toxic. That's why I tried so hard to suppress my reactions and not act on this inner static.

Sadly, most times... I just—could not—resist.

The child-abuse boot camp I endured conditioned me early on to never ask for assistance or relief—no matter the cost—feeding an unyielding desperation that silently disrupted my sense of self, well into my thirties.

On autopilot, I rushed through life as if there were a prize for finishing first. When I wasn't efficient, on time, or made even the smallest mistake—shit was about to go down.

Cue the incessant trepidation taking over. My mind spiraled into the worst case scenario—that everyone despised me and I was the most inept human who had ever graced the planet.

Messing up wasn't just an error that, more often than not, was common or easy to fix. Any mistake was a catastrophic betrayal of my existence.

Every ounce of mean spirited treatment felt deserved as I hoarded my self-loathing, turned the misery dial to max, and let my damnation gobble me up.

Time to assume the position to strangle myself into a downward spiral, leading me to believe that everyone hated me.

There unrested within...

The Beaten Dog Syndrome.

No matter how much torment withstood, I remained steadfast in my loyalty, attaching myself to anyone who gave me even the smallest scrap of attention. Only to drown in an abundance of hollow despair as those unbalanced relationships dragged me deeper into the abyss.

As if I were not low enough, I would always find a more hellish, chasmic hole to asphyxiate in, while I bled beneath the surface as I tried to keep calm and fake on.

Until the weight overran my hoax of unflappability, causing me to lash out in a wildly out-of-pocket and outlandish way.

To heighten the travail, I never knew anyone who was going through the same struggles which led me to feel that I had no one I could confide in. And once I tasted how easily people slap disapproved labels, and paint those in a bad light, I refused to open-up about my traumas to anyone.

So, what brought me temporarily out of my vicious cycle? My go-to-fix when the pressures of life infiltrated my nerves, grinding them unbearable?

With a *perfectly* polished exterior to the best of my ability, I hit the bar scene and got wasted for some short-lived, fake affection— a quick fix for an exiled spirit.

We can all agree that, when you mix drugs and alcohol with unhealed trauma and a scarred outlook—you do not get a party— you get a mess.

A. Hot. Mess. And nine times out of ten... that chaos incarnate was—*me.*

Seeing myself as a complete failure, I hopelessly sought consolation from others in all the wrong ways. It was a vicious, endless cycle, entirely of my own making.

There was a far-reaching deficit of certitude to love thyself, including the absence of fortitude to face my mirrored doppelgänger. I was unfit to admit that an emotional-support hype-squad would be integral to my survival.

Over time I learned that I thrived, felt alive, and seen whenever I received attention or recognition. It never mattered if it came from a man or a woman.

An ever-evolving emboldenment of my pseudo grew over time, fueling the healthy fats and carbs in my body—dramatizing my energy to keep me keepin' on.

Eventually, I came to understand—yet stubbornly ignored—the negative lack of help, love, positive guidance, or even the smallest act of reassurance—like a simple hug paired with *"Everything's going to be okay,"* fostered my first instinct to assist others.

Subconsciously, any level of kindness was priceless, deeply craved, and capable of breaking someone—this was the exact power that I handed over to everyone around me.

Restrained by the residue of trauma tripwires, I let others sculpt my worth. Tugging and yanking me around like their yo-yo—snapping me back under their grip.

This boundless care I embodied for others to lift them from their jaws of misery, was nowhere to be found when it came to respecting or encouraging myself.

Only for me to desert myself in the shadowlands of despair.

The simple feeling of being wanted, loved and useful—a modest *"Thank you"* or *"I appreciate you"*—was music to my ears that filled my heart with blissfulness until it faded away and I was hungry for more.

That benediction and fulfillment from others were like a drug to me—and a drug of choice—*it was.*

Once the glow of a good deed wore off, the fated hour of optimism descended, sending me spiraling into a depressed state. I stayed fettered by internal loathing, until there was something or someone that sparked a glimmer of hope, whispering for me to turn my back on the pain-I-felt-inside.

It was then time to mercilessly seek out others to spend time with to smother-the-sorrow.

On the flip side, I was never comfortable accepting help, gifts, or support. Acts of succor were something I was meant to provide, not receive.

The idea of others expending their energy on me was absurd—laughable, even. It was as if their time was too valuable to waste on the likes of me, as I mistakenly tried to handle it all by my lonesome.

The redundancy of my thoughtfulness—constant tool for seeking approval and gauging acceptance—was something I hitched onto in search of even the smallest shred of affirmation.

In hindsight, it's heartbreakingly sad to have lived that way—and painful, perhaps, for those who bore witness.

I was the Christopher Columbus of self-worthlessness, charting every unseamed coastline of expendability in a futile production to earn social niceties in the eyes of others.

Time to bottle up their kind feedback in a togo cup to sip on later—my little emotional morphine shot to ease my afflictions.

A snippet of joy to hold onto when my *"Can-do, life-is-great"* attitude inevitably got torn to shreds—like a hand in the waters of the Amazon Basin, ripped and shredded apart by fatal piranha bites.

This preserved interaction from others' compassion had a frustratingly short shelf life. Before I knew it my internal alarm went off, and I was back on the clock to assign my custom services to be doting on someone new.

Anyone else adjacent to me was fair game

as I set myself on fire to keep others warm in the chaos-of-life. All I had to do was coax out a teeny-tiny, sunshiny hint that I was doing something, *anything*—right.

"See?" I would tell myself, *"I am liked. I am needed. I am a good human being."*

The sad part? It worked for about five minutes.

Most folks like to call those enthralled with deciphering the desires of everyone a people-pleaser.

Whether it was to my face or behind my back, I was labeled as a brown-nosing, malleable person. Thanks to the crocodile smiles that *were* in my life.

Let me add my distinctive touch to the online definition of the...

Crocodile Smile:

"The kind of grin that masks unprincipled intentions so perfectly that the moment you turn your back, they will throw you under the bus and devour you alive.

Only to spit the 'insignificant bits' of you out—just enough to hug and kiss—leaving you in the dark, none the wiser, while they prime you up for their next nefarious pursuit—the next betrayal."

I knew, know, the people who used me or tried to from time to time. Every single one of them. But that didn't stop me from going out of my way for others. It stung being made fun of for it, sure, but it was my natural tendency, the only way I knew.

Putting others first wasn't just a habit— it was the glue holding my puzzle-pieced mind together, so I didn't shatter apart like a windshield in a fatal car crash.

Did I have remorse when I over-promised an assist? Absolutely—I had plenty. But no matter what, my word has always been my honor, and that is one thing I refuse to break.

Without hesitation, I offered to carry the weight of others—far beyond what anyone asked for or even implied. Hell, most of the time, nothing was requested.

But there I was, stepping in, just for the slim chance to win their good graces and earn a throwaway, cordial, verbal gesture. More often than not, it bit me in the ass.

Let's be real, some could care less about the reasons behind people-pleasing.

Why should they? They get what they want without even asking for it, in my case, making their lives easier with a good laugh at the same time.

Then, there's the crowd that presumes people-pleasers are too clueless they're being used.

Guess again. We notice—*I noticed.*

Back then, I couldn't afford to face that level of pain. I had neither the self-respect nor love for myself to even deliberate upon it.

The first thing someone usually sees is someone unworthy and anguished for attention or acceptance. Which, there's truth in that judgment—ensnared deep within my chaotic thought process.

But does anyone ever stop to ask why? Does anybody even care? Why is it that some of us can't nurture ourselves, yet we will break-our-necks to cater to others' wishes?

Being a yes-woman for me was a silent flare in the fog, not realizing I was doing it in the first place. I was one who never expected anything of monetary value—most certainly no strings attached—but, as we all know, not everyone has a selfless endgame.

Avenging others' misdeeds? Always, I was practically raised on that doctrine. Disrespect seems to hit differently when you have been mistreated as a child.

Whoever was ill-mannered, cheated, lied, harassed—you name it—I lost my shit. I even stuck my nose where it didn't belong to ensure justice was served. I only let things slide once they owned up to their actions, apologized, and made things right.

Otherwise, let's just say, I lean hard into my unsolicited accountability tendencies.

My knee-jerk reaction to hold people

answerable to conscience—ahem, 'Karen'—stemmed from me not standing up decisively for myself. To be fair, I didn't hand out the full pummeling and tongue-lashings for others to see it through, either.

I have always been the type to voice my endless opinions of right and wrong, usually with zero filter back in the day. Now? Let's call it a crapshoot. I teeter-totter between composed and on-point—to kicking myself firmly in my mouth.

On a more prominent note, I was quieter in complex situations, like corporate settings. I tried to be diplomatic and not cause *too* much of a problem. That was—until—the one in line to be the top brass of a cut-throat organization hit harsh levels of misconduct.

Here's the thing... those high-ups were playing Chess like grandmasters while I was over here trying to figure out the rules of Go Fish using UNO cards.

These Bears that I am trying to verbally poke, prod and accost, didn't just have a head start—they were already at the finish line, sipping champagne and eating caviar as they laughed at my uneducated training wheels.

Chapped-Man would licentiously press his expanding penis on my right shoulder and back area as he stood behind me at my computer and leaned forward. Since he doesn't like to be ignored, he chose to *waterboard* me with vindictive oversight, as he inundated me with insolent, impudent, and imprudent debauchery when I tried to stand up for myself.

All while Natta-Tara bolstered the CEO in-line's blue-balls crusade, by blackballing me in the choppy corporate seas of the Shaky-Ground Bay Area.

Chapped-Man joined forces to seal some shady backroom deal—tied a cement block around my ankles and threw me overboard in shark-infested waters.

Like galvanic corrosion, I was metal left in saltwater, never rinsed clean—slowly cracking in a low-healing environment, putrefying inward without boundaries under Death Valley's scorching heat.

An overwhelming, burnout-born of self-doubt totalized my senses—flooding me with raw, impulsive stresses both uniform and pitting against my naïveté.

Which is super-shitty, since they always seem to win. And sure, picking my battles and knowing when to walk away would be the obvious curriculum of consequence—potentially or logically even, it would be the most meaningful lesson to learn.

Or maybe it's taking a stab at playing the long game? We shall see... hee—*hee.*

I literally pucker and shrivel up like a raisin when someone yells, whether near me or worse—at me. My entire being retreats into a dark, airless box with no escape, shutting down without a shred of emotional endurance or inner guardrails to guide me back to safety.

In my youth, best believe this-bitch would fight or yell right back. Only for my fight-or-flight instincts to not know what to do.

My mind would be stuck in the middle of those pent-up emotions—angel and devil on each shoulder going at it.

Now the older, more mature, and calmer me just wants the situation to evaporate and leave everything in God's hands. No drama, no yelling—just a quick exit, please and thank you.

When it's aimed at me nowadays, I walk away rattled for a minute, replay it, and then—voilà—it's gone. If it's others hashing things out, I either try to mediate or back off and hope they figure it out without pulling me in.

Back then, the worst part? I convinced myself that the ill-intended behavior was justified. That night, the next day, or even years later, my brain would replay the whole cluster f*ck on a loop—start to finish, forevermore.

Self-throwing wrenches at this here wench, came as naturally to me as walking.

One foot in front of the other—straight into my own oversights—with no delights.

My fixating, over-dissecting, and insecure self always managed to cover all the bases, including the inconceivable ones. But hey, it's hard to surprise me when I have run through all the thinkable scenarios—even the ridiculous ones no one else would consider.

Not once did speaking up pay me dividends. It slips into the well-worn cracks of business-as-usual anomie.

Like the time the youngest Partner at a CPA firm in San Mateo, California— Galli, Thomps & Flow-Cuss—smacked me on the butt with a screwdriver while I filed client documents. I was only twenty-years old or so at the time.

When I asked the older women in the office why I was let go they said, *"It's just politics. You will understand when you are older and more experienced."*

Usher in the self-degradation: *"Yes Missy, you're the f*ck-up. The unlikable one who will* *never measure up."*

One thing I excelled at was being my own worst enemy. The blame landed squarely on me—because, of course, I should have known better than to call out harassment from the executives I supported.

Never mind the tangled web of joint action entwinement that extends to the likes of a diverse range of companies, by way of example and not limitation: Apple, Norton, Lookout, FedEx, AT&T, Xfinity, OpenAI and JPMorgan Chase.

Being in public was exhausting if I was sober. Alcohol wasn't just a social lubricant—it was a lifeline.

To soften the discomfort of living in my own skin, flooding my bloodstream with neurochemical agents was quintessential. So my brain wouldn't ricochet like hockey pucks, banged-out non-stop in some endless practice round of life.

It was vital to be hyper-aware of every little thing around me, so that I could assess personalities alongside their behaviors.

My mind ran on relentless over drive, unraveling its mental entanglements over every nuance in the fine print of life.

Substances were the key to temporary relief, drowning out the steaming-hot, noggin-noodle soup commentary.

This sedated sanctuary welded my mental toolbox shut and short-circuited the rest, saving me from driving myself completely nuts. Of course, this escape came with its own problems—some mornings I woke up jammed with a rusted memory of the night before... *yikes.*

By eighteen, approbation for myself was categorically non-existent.

In striking divergence, all my reverence, warm-heartedness, and boundless positivity were lavished on any, and everyone—else.

Besotted-by-the-bottle and stuffing my face with food, had me blowing up like Violet from Willy Wonka. One bottle of vino went down as easily as a tic-tac. On the rare event

I skipped the hard stuff, even two flagons of fermented grapes felt as juvenile as poppin' bubbles with cigarette-shaped gum.

Obsessed with shedding the weight I had stacked on seemingly overnight, keen to try anything and everything to turn back time. When a new diet pill that hit the shelves— sign me up. Let's not leave out that enticing weight-loss classic... cocaine.

At barely sixteen, my soon-to-be boyfriend was fifteen years my senior and more than willing to feed my cravings. The result was a comatose version of me, blind to who he really was and what the f*ck was going on.

Given that I am athletic and played most sports growing up, I never tried the gym back then. Why bother when I could take the quick-fix, effortless route?

One that afforded me playtime to mingle-n-tease in misbehaves of the frolicky kind.

Typically, I was wasted, buzzed, or hungover. Drained of any motivation to move, let alone thrive. All my energy went into maintaining an 'immaculate' exterior: makeup on point, hair flawless—because if nothing else, I should at least, look-the-part.

Daddy-Dearest was the grand poohbah of negative self-talk, and the catalyst that taught me this self-sabotaging chatter.

Compromisingly, I teared myself down every second of the day. Whether it was during interactions, errands, or just existing. I was my own wrecking ball demolition crew, with no one else in the driver's seat but *me*.

My fake confidence laid waste to the point where I was a stranger to myself. No more familiar than an alien or blood sucking reptilian in human cloak, slithering past me on a crowded street.

Compliments from family or friends never truly mattered. Even if their kind words briefly warmed me. Their pats on the back did not register, since I was incapable of seeing or feeling the truth in what they saw.

Those fleeting moments of reassurance were like pouring water into a dying plant infested with spider mites, fungus gnats, aphids, and every other pest imaginable. Doomed to wither until the root causes in my shackled mentality were addressed.

When I stepped through the trembling veil to fix myself, it was purely superficial. Solely my outer appearance to mask any shortcomings. One blemish—no matter how small—was enough to send me spiraling into freak out mode, as if that single flaw defined my entire worth.

No stone went unturned in my manic quest to patch up every cosmetic defect. One imperfection ruined my entire day. Whatever I presented to the world had to be 'flawless.' A sharp contrast to how I was on the inside— obliterated, bordering-beyond repair.

Real goals? My only ambition was to hold down a respectable job. No small feat for someone who surprisingly passed middle school and dropped out of high school.

There was no rhyme or reason, in any of my seasons. But hey, shout out to the

California education system for passing an almost straight F-and-D student all the way until I walked away.

I shuffled through five different high schools before quitting about two months into my junior year at sixteen. Straight to the real-world, where I racked up twenty-four years of adulting by cramming one or two positions in the eleven industries I dabbled in.

My prime was a frenzied henroost—drug induced and seduced. I recklessly stumbled wherever the wind blew me—usually off another steep bank, outranked by my empty think-tank.

Boy, do I got stories. I flipped and flopped like a fish outta-wattah, sippin' that fire water. While some tried to crack this noggin with a hammer or step on me.

When it came to accomplishments, jacks-diddly came to mind. In my eyes, there was nothing for me to be proud of. All because I constantly compared myself to everyone else. Especially when stacked against that family member who seemed to have it all together.

This warped takeaway left me falling short, cast as the habitual f*ck-up. It felt like the cold-hard-truth since eighty percent of the time I found all the ways to exacerbate the 50/50 chance wrong.

Life has been like me dragging myself by the throat through broken glass, collecting septic debris in my old, open wounds. Each shard birthed infections that chipped away at my soul, as it slapped me upside the head and drained my stream of animus.

Forsaking thee before allowing myself adequate time to flourish—leaving me discarded-and-deprived.

In my late twenties, around 2012, I went to community college to expand thy wisdom.

Okay, okay... expand—thy—pea-brain.

Working at my first public company ("Site-Oh"), inspired me to dedicate myself by investing in my education. The exposure in that role and a specific co-worker lit the spark for a couple of semesters.

Those opened doors filled me with aspirations, and maybe a touch of greed since I wanted to climb the ladder faster with a specific career in mind.

The idea of jumping ship was irresistible. A chance to snag a new bag of tricks at my short stint in corporate. What I did not expect was to land in positions that offered lessons no book could ever teach and ones you would not hear about in conversation.

Leaving Site-Oh's port, my eyes were fanatical to be nautical. With sails set to conquer uncharted seas, I jammed to my sea shanties. Navigating through a couple of mentally fatal companies, my deck took on more water than I bargained for.

They capsized and disenfranchised me while holding me under. Only to scrutinize and patronize with nothing but lies. I finally left them ill-advised and sensitized.

One of the many things I have never denied was adding another notch to my multi-faceted belt. I was predominantly agreeable to test most things once—never knowing when I might need to **fill-that-gap,** or let it **all-hang-out.**

Living unreservedly in my head, worried about the views of others while I tried to mask everything under the sun, trained me to overthink the lock, stock, and barrel of things. It's remarkable that I never triggered migraines from the constant fireworks I ignited in my cerebral cortex.

This ability to replay moments where I justified myself with the speed of greased lightning—only to relive them years later—was maddening.

The number of times I explained, every—little—thing—down to the most trifling details, was my very own public service announcement on how woefully unwise and ineffective I was.

Words spilled out like a dam breaking,

flooding every space with explanations and unnecessary confessions, leaving others drowning in information overload. With the silent awkwardness of no one speaking in return is outright painful.

Admittedly, it still gets me at times. I am an evolving saga, constantly polishing myself in the margins of these exchanges.

Not a single favor was returned for the energy I poured into whatever I rambled on about. Faces would start to glaze over, responses were cut short as if I were speaking a language only I understood.

For the life of me, I could not figure out what I was missing. What invisible code everyone else had cracked while I was left chasing my avalanche of words.

The harsh, double-edged truth about relationships is this: people thrive on shared experiences, both struggles and successes.

Trust is rooted in honesty, and grows from a true sense of belonging, shaped by those who value and accept me for who I am—

a safety net of unalloyed connections.

Legitimate friendships are not going to blossom if I am falling over myself to be saluted and can't trust or respect myself—and-then-some.

Back then, I over-divulged and trusted too easily. My exertions to stay relevant or fit-in backfired, leaving me seen as expendable. I tried so hard that, ironically, I reduced myself to being nothing more than a glitch in their personal cosmos.

Infinite times I face planted straight into the mouth of a Florida swamp—in the dead summer heat—leaving me beat, with no one to greet.

I was the book that collected dust on a shelf, only to be picked up and thumbed through when it was convenient for the beholder. A prop for them to look busy, curb boredom, or serve as a placeholder while they eavesdropped on something better.

Sadly, I was terrible in conversations if I wasn't interested in the topic, scared to voice my opinion, or my mind wandered off in the fourth dimension. I then grew mute and awkward.

That's when my ticking time bomb of a brain would start the countdown, ready to detonate if I could not find a way to reinsert myself into the discussion.

More often than not, I was the runaway train-of-words—a blabbering fool—trying to prove some inconsequential point or angle, impatiently needing to be right about something.

Looking back, I wish someone had just cut me off with a playful *"Get to the point!"* Or teased, *"Oh, of course you know... please— do explain!"*

Although that's exactly what I needed to hear, no one was ever up for the arduous task of telling me. Either they feared it might cause unease in the relationship, or it is more likely—they were **not**—my true—friends.

I, however, would have curtsied to the wake-up call. Every lesson in humility I have endured, cracked the innate shell of my self-myth—no matter how eye-rolling annoyed, I was.

Begrudgingly, functioning through life, I only illustrated what I perceived others wanted me to represent. Often, I was told that I resembled a chameleon by fitting into various cliques.

While I succeeded in blending in with others' quests and hobbies swimmingly, I never genuinely held a place.

Thanks to the intrinsic need to fit in with whoever crossed my path, I was curated into being exceptionally well-rounded, even as I struggled to acknowledge who I was.

CATCH-22: I couldn't accept or love myself because I didn't know who I was—and I couldn't know who I was without first accepting myself.

If someone liked me, or so I sensed, I questioned why? Instead of being biddable to it, I would run the other way doubting their objective while spiraling into an uncomfortable state of mind about being fancied. I kept everyone at a distance, locked out by my impenetrable, emotional walls.

For the most part, I surrounded myself with crocodile acquaintances who were not sincere or loyal companions. I was their unfeigned stand-in when they either needed something from me or their real friends were unavailable.

Meanwhile, I overlooked the kindred spirits who could have been my true confidants.

Refusing to see the propitious side of the bright-'n'-kind folk who entered my sunlight, I snubbed the possibility that not everyone had ulterior motives.

Instead, I cradled my refusal to take care of my mental health and quality of life— a wretched way to live.

'Insert-dramatic-throat-clear-here.'

I acted this way because, well... that was exactly Dad's modus operandi.

The bitter irony? I spent so much time convincing myself that I was the polished one, the one who held her tongue more than Pops ever did.

But me keeping quiet was piddling at best. Sighs-and-eyes, advise.

It was a tough pill to swallow, very humbling to say the least, on how much I mirrored the very things I hated. The man I despised for so many years, the one whose mere life disgusted me for the way he treated me and others—turns out, I had inherited more than I cared to surrender out loud.

And yet, I was not just fighting him— I was fighting the fact that I was turning into a mutated version of his—mini-me.

So, what snapped me out of it?

Well, Mom finally had enough of my outbursts. She was over me flying off the handle, freaking out, distressed whenever things were not taken as seriously as I expected them to be—or performed to my impossible standard of *perfection*.

Dad's voice echoed in my head: *"The most consistent thing in life is... people will always disappoint you. Want something done right? Do it yourself. Do it right the first time... that's not how it's done— give me that, I will do it!"*

Growing up, I saw the world the same way I saw myself—harshly. I expected everyone to give 111%, take pride in their work by caring about the details, otherwise, what's the point?

Forsaking my own lane, I drowned in waters too deep, all while mandating others to meet my thresholds while tacking on, *"You can't complain unless you gave a genuine effort."*

As my mottled brain slowly decayed, I choked on the idea to remember others' likes and dislikes, to demonstrate respect, and to meet halfway.

Mom's response—and the look on her face—will forever be seared into my inner universe when she said, *"Sometimes, you are really like your father."*

When she called me out, I whipped my head whiplash fast, as if I was trying to snap my own neck to end my cautionary tale.

At the same time, my jaw practically hit the floor as I walked away—zapped by a stun gun—*stunned.*

That warning shot left me in a cataleptic trance, overwhelmed with emotion.

My brain hit the emergency brakes as I blew through the rail and stalled my car on the train tracks. A near death-dealing-blow, that needed a few days to marinate in my gray matter—leaving me utterly devoid of any level of justification.

Then came the *"Oh f*ck, she is right!"* Hitting me where no one has had the guts to go.

Not just a realization—it was the 'Mack-Truck-of-Truth,' obliterating my carefully crafted delusions. A truth so mind altering, I do not have the words to describe it. I was unable to see it before because I was a self-appointed peepin' Tam, spying on the flaws of every Tom, Dick, and Harry out there.

My ornery ass did not have the moxie to face myself. I was laser-focused on everyone else, except for the one person who truly matters to me—*me*.

I was—I am—I will always be, my only obligation.

Denying my festering trauma escorted me into a life of sleepwalking through my tipsy continuance, as I turned my bare face quietly away from the truth. This torpid state cocooned me from self-development and accountability—an evasion of my own becoming.

Life was a compiled blur of days so desensitized by sedatives, narcotics, and hooch—no specific memory stands out. An endless loop of numbing myself into a negligent, comfort zone.

Enough was finally—*enough*. It was time—past time—to put an end to my decades late, hundreds-of-thousand of dollars short—life.

My heart was beating, but I was barely alive. Almost on my last breaths... but wait, I am ready to breathe for the first time.

See-Truetles—Says-Toodles, to my former legacy of lackadaisically chillin' like a sloth as I clutched-at-straws in my self-medicated hideout—shroud-playing as if I had this whole life thing all figured out.

In my erstwhile, f*cked-up reality—the only thing I had mastered was:

Riding-the-Waves of Pleasure Town.

Bout' time I found a pair of adult woman pants that fit, buckled my buttercup the f*ck up and stopped lying to myself—because funny enough, I never outwardly lied to anyone else once I entered the real-world.

And so, that good-for-nothing defeatist mentality overstayed its lousy welcome.

That unfortunate hand dealt to me as a kiddo? It was getting older and more tiresome than the deception of our world—no longer a valid play for either.

Come on now, I am well past childhood. This act is a fossil that should have gone extinct ages ago.

There is no more bandwidth to confuse this simulation by running amok in a third dimensional falsehood. Time to log out of denial and face what I am truly made of.

Moping around yet not taking adequate action while concealing the trueness of it all—left me playing games with my mind like a complete imbecile.

After so many tries, I reached a breaking point—my last race to catch the salubrity train to shatter my insanity-driven cycle through the reframing of myself.

This wild apple was ready to take a healthy bite out of life. My inner drums began to beat a harmoniously dignified tune, blaring my newfound rhythm into a white-light state of consciousness.

Almost as if magical gloves are gently guiding me, unveiling new creations within and steering me closer to my true calling.

Not to kid around with my philosophical, sunshine-and-rainbows talk—this road to a newfangled line of thinking did not happen overnight.

It took time and grit to stomach and persevere through some vile—dreadfully-draining-durations—all while resisting my first instinct to relapse into a waste-case, undermining whatever progress I procured.

There was no volition within me but to be wholeheartedly devoted to myself—exactly the way I had been to everyone else.

Once and for all, I had to face the truth: these personality-ulcers were no longer sustainable. It was time to drag my butt to the drawing board, armed with a no-holds-barred initiative to refashion my everything.

To make this achievable, the first step was to discard everything I thought I knew, while disavowing the toxic matrix I had been sucked into.

Next came—*acceptance.*

When I welcomed my life, forgave father, and worked to exculpate myself, I unlocked the ability to learn how to truly love myself—authentically and unapologetically—before offering helping hands to anyone else.

Each daybreak I am blessed to wake and bring a renewed resurgence—a call to end this self-harm and commit to restructuring my life.

The indomitable drive to succeed in this life is no longer optional—it's non-negotiable, every... day.

This was an exigent decision. One that required me to summon the stamina of will, one way or another.

Life is too precious—too valuable—for me to squander.

Now that I find myself diligently engaged in revamping my world in this new galaxy, I have become one with the act of indagating the phenomenal vivacity within me, toward the infinite potential ahead.

Eradicating my comfort zone to pursue my passion as a Wordsmith, has been an exceedingly mind-breaking journey into the unknown.

My legs are buckling on a wet sailboat deck as I travel across the world without a compass, trying to find my way.

By the grace of God, it has proven to be the most rewarding endeavor when all is said and done—but it has also been an isolating and lonely voyage.

Countless moments—then and now—leave me unraveling, as I silently whisper to God: *"Who will want to buy my memoir? Why would anyone care? Who am I to think I can help or inspire someone?"*

After a bit of time passes, I take a few deep breaths to ground myself and remember why I chose to lay myself bare—to be this transparently vulnerable in the first place.

Writing a hundred hours a week feels like eight—utterly effortless. It galvanizes and sparks my soul, propelling me to heights I never foresaw as a realistic avenue for myself, all while passionately inspiring me to keep moving forward.

Sentence-slinging as a text tactician feels like my true calling. It's a creative lifeline, serving as both my sole source of pizzazz and the purest outlet pulsing through my core and beyond.

It's time to build a better life—one that is centered around doing what I love. A life where I wake up each day with purpose, fueled by passion—recharging my inner battery, and driving the determination to keep on truckin' toward my dreams.

This enhanced life will be brought to fruition when I reach the level of expertise as a 'Wordipulator.'

Looks as though this word has not been established or widely used—and if it has, I missed it.

Regardless, I define it as: the Principal Architect of Articulation—rearranging letters with mischief and *surgical* precision.

Tremendous ideas are brewing within, like Mentos shaken in a soda bottle, erupting into dynamic masterpieces through the artful manipulation of the alphabet.

There have been some derailments that test my resolve, working hard to wear down my patience. The goal is to translate these into opportunities for a deeper sense of enlightenment, nudging me toward elevated discernment and depth for the next time around, as dilemmas will be inevitable.

Every day, I look forward to broadening my worldview, knowing it draws me closer to my next project—a limitless work of fiction—where my imagination will know, *no* bounds.

Time to pierce the veil of hesitation and bash-on regardless—embracing all hours that I am... blessed-to-live.

Light Switch Mentality

The euphoric escape I encountered from alcohol and schedule two's, rapidly flipped the light switch on and off in my cognitive pathways.

Electric waves coursed through me—sedating my mind, body, and soul.

My sole intention was to be enchanted and illuminated in a dream state, even if only for a brief flicker-of-time, before my mind dilapidated into a dark consciousness.

The preponderant of my existence was depleted while I chased that charged feeling, transiently filling the void that cursed me.

There were blipped seconds when I tried to cut off this light to my forbidden escape, seeking healthier paths toward healing.

But, like a moth to Edison's luminous orb, my thermal energy inevitably attracted dark souls.

These sparked connections activated an electric surge of emotions, only for my light bulb to pop and snuff out without a trace.

In time, I began to justify cutting corners when I patched up the frayed wires in my fuse box with dirty, foul—duds.

My floodlights only turned on when I blacked-out my perplexities, paving the way to a lightning strike of dopamine and serotonin—a fugacious high that only fortified my false sense of reality.

When the Truth Erupts... What If?!

At times, the very breaths I breathed left me longing for understanding, my mind bespread with what might have been.

Given that my brain was conditioned to accept abuse as though I deserved it, I schlepped myself down an unmentionable, agonizing path.

It discomforts me to say that—most of my life—I truly didn't care about my health or future.

This was a thoughtless, train-wreck of a mindset that catapulted me into a reckless existence, seething in the depths of a maelstrom.

I was over the moon for new beginnings whether real or imagined. Desperate to erase the echoes of past mistakes and the haunting trials of tribulation. I yearned for a clean slate to create something meaningful for myself. Or at least, to pretend my life had never been what it was.

To embody this type of mental state for so many years feels like undue torture in retrospect. Unquestionably, I am thankful I no longer recognize any part of that 'Young Mo,' nor am I connected to that radioactive, cognitive labyrinth.

That road is one—I will never—trudge *again.*

In my unhealed state, I often wondered what life would have been like if Dad raised me in a nurturing environment filled with patience, love and respect.

Where the cruelty of abuse was as foreign as being handed a dictionary to search for an unrecorded word that was unspoken and unrelatable to anyone, anywhere.

A world so harmonious that only radiant and uplifting notions fueled my reasoning mechanism.

But then I would spiral into a double-sided purgatory of the mind, convinced that no matter what goals I formed—yet never acted upon or tried to change—I would declare, *"I will never be good enough. So why bother?"*

Why should I push past a surface level front? It is way easier for me to reject all that pain-I-feel-inside. Not like I care that it's chipping away at my soul like a pickaxe, obliterating a delicate flower bed.

This here mental tapestry relentlessly weaved hypothetical, what-if scenarios for stupendous new ways for me to break inwardly as if I harbored a personal vendetta against my sanity.

Poignantly enough, these ideas barged in when everything was tickety-boo. That's when it became time to shove my inner self back down into my so-called comfy, yet comprehensively miserable state of self-doubt *where I belonged.*

A treacherous terrain that most shoes

would not dare to tread.

I could never allow myself a brief stint of chirpiness. My neurologically damaged brain itched for a quick flash of something jarring to wipe away those fairy-tailed, peaches-and-cream, dreams.

Stopping mid-thought was never an option until my chest caved in, squeezing the life out of my heart—*hooray*—a single tear crept down my defiled face, scuttling me into my so-called... *safe-space*.

My psyche always needed to run away from consistent, long-term feelings of happy-go-lucky affections, as earnestly joyful beliefs left me feeling awkward. I was unequipped to appreciate them on a permanent basis— it was too movie-fake for me to be in that type of fantasy world.

Anything lovie-dovie, forget about it. There must be some dysfunction, action thrillers and horror only for me, please.

During the times when I personified inner-soul-shine, it left me completely off kilter, acting peculiarly in that "*I have no idea how to handle this,*" kind of way.

The natural upside-down instincts would kick in, blowing out my candle of life, as I nitpicked an already over-thunk thought a couple more times—times a few.

Like most repetitive day-to-day chores that become boring, my real-life flashbacks stopped doing the trick to snap me out of these love-like feelings.

My brain would solicit extensive harm, from the worst-case scenario, to how an idolized life could go horribly wrong.

Footprints of days past would scratch the parietal lobe of my neural dance, reminding me that it no longer had the desired effect— that I needed to take it further. It was time to bring on the psychopathic destruction to the forefront of my cerebral mantle.

From there, I would cogitate on me not being around anymore, and all the *fun,* **hypothetical, speculative,** what-if questions that come with the following ideation's:

What if I died tragically? Would anyone notice I was gone? Miss me? Think of me?

What if no one plans a funeral? What if no one attends my wake?

What if everyone forgot I was ever on Earth in the first place?

What if no one would shed a tear if they never saw me again?

What if no one pays tribute to my passing on social media on the anniversary, my birthday or at any point in time?

When those speculative ideas of not being around anymore pierced my heart, only to quickly lose their sting, my mind would pivot to the 'positive side.'

What if I am not completely delusional and I will accomplish something meaningful?

What if Dad raised me in a well-adjusted, white-picket-fence family?

What if Pops sat me down at the dinner table and had healthy, constructive conversations instead of dysfunction?

What if I applied myself and excelled in school?

What if I had been the starting catcher on a softball team at a well-respected University, earned a bachelor's in English with a minor in Psychology, and then went on to law school?

What if I had learned from my mistakes instead of letting them consume me?

What if I every little slip-up wasn't the be-all and end-all of my existence?

What if my parents were happily married or amicably divorced?

What if Pops never put Mom down in front of me or traumatized her as well?

What if Mom cheated and my *'real'* father is somewhere out there?

What if Pops explained to me how men should properly treat women, and led by example as a model parent?

What if Dad respected and valued me?

What if the Old Man hugged me regularly, spoke to me about life with patience and care, explaining it thoroughly, calmly, and appropriately?

Now, for the explicit, unfiltered truth on how my life came crashing down.

What if I am done getting my turtle-dove feathers ruffled now that I am reclaiming my dignity as I find my voice—truth-locked and word-loaded, ready to pluck the Pelican's feathers the f*ck out?

What if a town wields so much power that it can manipulate local and national *'news'* networks?

What if someone died during a game that was broadcast globally—a tragedy I witnessed with my own eyes? I know their fault, the part they played, but it will never make the news.

No one would provoke their destiny by publicizing this de facto shadow authorities' criminal dealings, because crossing them means they will—f*ck—your—life—up.

What if whoever shined a red sniper light on my chest while I stood in the living room, with coffee in hand to scare me into silence—**never-going-to-f*chin'-happen.** Was anonymously revealed and the scales of justice tip in the honorable, law-abiding direction?

What if a well-known general contractor in Monterey—proud owner of a about twenty Indian motorcycles—did not renege on his word to assist me with the Monterey Police?

What if this general contractor said, *"I have a friend who is an FBI agent that lives in Pebble Beach, I will ask him to help you."*

What if this corrupt, dirty-ass, pathetic excuse for a human—I mean—what if this FBI agent was not involved, and actually held the Monterey Police beholden to truth?

Alas, so sad for me, after the contractor talked with this FBI agent, he said *"Sorry, I can't help you. I have too much to lose."*

What if this FBI agent—residing in Pebble Beach—turned out to be none other than the head Pelican I reported to the Monterey Police and in my internet crimes submission to the FBI?

What if one Pelican, by which I mean the foul Badge-scum, lawyers, mayor, anyone who played a part is wrapped in my Pelican blanket name—decided to morph into a duck, and quack-quacks the truth to save-their-own-ass-while-on-Earth?

What if these Pelicans Tellin' Porkies were subject to scrutiny for abusing their government resources to spy on and threaten innocent citizens—not just me—all for their own personal gain?

What if Lieutenant Jake Pinkas of the Monterey Police respected his duties and did not shun the email I sent him mid-to-late March 2023?

A plea that is now, oh-so-conveniently deleted from my account. In it, I asked what my options were to reinstate the complaint I originally filed against Richard Castellon and Jesse Phillips on February 9, 2023.

What if I didn't cancel the complaint on February 13, 2023, due to the sheer terror from death threats as they hijacked my world and destabilized me... piece-by-piece?

What if the Monterey Police did not sit there in amusement due to their severe lack of rectitude, negation of human decency, and atrocities perpetrated against my civil rights and life?

What if the Pelicans figured out I have the email they erased from my account? The one Mike Garcia of the Monterey Police sent me on September 12, 2023, at 10:50 AM PT:

"Hello Monique, How can I help you? I hope you're in a place where you feel safe, and yes, there are a lot of strange and suspect people out there. Remember, you are doing the right thing by standing up and saying something. It's not always easy being the whistleblower, but hang in there."

The Pelicans underestimated just how paranoid their digital threats, gross edits and deletions of my writing made me. I saved that email in more places than I could even keep track of.

What if the Pelicans learned that I cracked the code to Mike Garcia's role in all of this—and why he probably tripped the wire of his own making for sending that email calling me a whistleblower?

Maybe that's why they made it vanish from my account—to erase any proof it existed.

Bad Cops—Bad Cops...

Whatcha Gunna Do?

Whatcha Gunna Do... When-I-Come-For-You?

To state the obvious—it will be legal and ethical.

What if Elliott from the San Jose U.S. Marshals gave one flying shit when I called him about five times and emailed him once, using the generic email he gave me?

Elliott asked for the name of the so-called Marshal who came to my house and seized—stole—digital documentation, handwritten notes, and disposable cameras constituting evidence against FISA abuse by an FBI agent and conspirators?

What if Elliott had actually earned his taxpayer-funded salary and ordered the Monterey Police—along with everyone else involved—to be investigated and indicted for 'playing along' with the impersonation of a Federal Agent?

Instead, Elliott chose to hang up on me, parroting an FBI canned response—hoping I would stop *saying things* on the US Marshals recorded line.

What if for once, someone in our government stood up and did the right thing?

Department of Justice complaints ("DOJ") and Freedom of Information Act requests ("FOIA") were filed in March 2025—filing federal complaints or requests under false pretenses can land you five years behind bars, per offense.

No one in their right mind risks twenty-years of their prime unless they're telling the explicit, God's honest truth.

However, the DOJ has outright ignored the complaints. To me, that signals that they approve of police officer's invoking federal authority to rob American citizens.

I have a sneaky suspicion, though, that if I ever impersonated a United States Federal Marshal, the consequences would be swift and unforgiving.

The *funniest* part?

FOIA for the Marshal's cited subsection 7(f), claiming that releasing their internal communications about my conversations or complaints would *"endanger someone's life."*

The only people present or involved other than me were the Monterey Police in-person, and then a week later—US Marshal Elliott over the phone.

To me, that reads as if disclosure would put my life in danger—since I am the victim, and only government players are involved— and there was **never** an investigation.

7(F) is a semantic, 'legal' loophole game meant to frustrate anyone who questions the government's illegality, and is weaponized to exhaust the requestor.

The DOJ's utter failures to legally respond constitutes an improper withholding under 5 U.S.C. § 552(a)(4)(B) and reflect an arbitrary, capricious, and constructive denial of appeals, in direct violation of their non-descretionary, statutory obligations.

Apparently, they're protecting corrupt government employees, the Monterey Police, and the 'Private Party' involved.

Literally, the only play I have left is to be the twisted-thorn branches in their assholes until this is rectified.

Whether it's the DOJ, FBI, US Marshal's—whomever's burden shall be my sanctity, because the truth is combustible—a wildfire consuming lies and deceitful cover-ups.

What if Merrill Lynch's SVP, Russ Upton, was paid to befriend me or had skin in the game?

The way Russ came at me—trying to catch me slippin' at the Carmel Valley Ranch bar around August 5, 2022, spitting golf stories like bait on a hook, daring me to break the so-called *legal* NDA with that 'Private Party.'

This wasn't a social conversation over drinks, burgers, tuna and french fries—it was a calculated gambit to compel repayment of settlement monies.

Then Russ dropped, *"What do you think my friend meant when she said, I finally feel free, alive and anxious about living my life?"*

Interesting. That is the exact opening to my book—word for word. It wasn't until everyone else started dropping lines from my life that I began piecing it together: how many people had read my unpublished, private work—watched me—spied-on-me.

And sometimes I stare in the ineffable—was the guy I reported to the Monterey Police and FBI, one of Russ's clients from his ultra-high-net-worth book of business at Merrill Lynch?

What if Gloria Allred's law firm—Allred, Maroko & Goldberg—was up to date with California law with respect to NDAs?

If they were, I highly suspect they would have refused the agreement provided by the opposing party since it violated the STAND Act, which took effect on January 1, 2019.

Although, I was given no other option but to sign the NDA without reading it in December 2019.

What if Gloria Allred's team had not rushed me through the process?

They gave me a watered-down, abridged version because they were in a hurry to leave. Had I known what was really in that NDA, there's no way I would have signed the coerced document.

Then again... what if Allred's team was fully up to date on the STAND Act—but they didn't bother to read the NDA, and pressured me to sign it in less than a minute since they could have given a shit less—was their loyalty *not* to me?

Or worse: what if they read it, and in cold calculation, chose to safeguard the opposing parties' interests rather than my own?

"Plaintiff will simply state 'the matter has been resolved' and will make no other comments... Plaintiff agrees not to make any public statements, or any statements which she reasonably believes are likely to become public, whether written, oral or electronic, which statements could be interpreted under the circumstances as embarrassing, disparaging, prejudicial or in any way detrimental to the interests of the COMPANY."

What if Dolores—Allred's employee— hadn't abandoned me when I told her, *"I can't take it anymore,"* especially after she had said, *"Let us know how we can help."* When I pointed out that the other party had breached the contract based on the verbal summary upchucked at the time of the cornered signing?

What if Dolores did not constructively desert me when it was clear the de facto shadow authority was retaliating for revenge?

What if I hurt some 'big boy' egos by staying in Monterey with those... dolla' dolla' billz' ya'll?!

What if the Monterey Police told Derail and Cat that I lost my rocker after I confided in another family member about a sniper red light aimed on my chest, and that it was not safe to be in the house?

What if Derail and Cat concluded I wasn't important enough to be spied on, conveniently ignoring the fact that I signed a non-disclosure with powerful Pelicans?

What if Derail said he is friends with the CIA agent who went against the agency and was sent to prison for years—later wrote a book about it?

Derail mentioned that this agent's training had strengthened his chances of survival while incarcerated, and that the same agent planned to write the foreword for Derail's book to lend it credibility.

What if I talked to Chari, Cat's sister, and Chari said she was not surprised by what happened to me? 237

What if Chari told me that Cat had her arrested as well—for a sisterly disagreement—which is one of the many reasons why they don't talk to each other?

What if Chari went on to explain that both Cat and Derail have a long history of being kicked-out-of-churches because of their manipulation and fabricated stories?

What if Cat and Derail's psychosomatic—fake therapist—self-help bullshit they push on people, not just me, hadn't distracted the Monterey Police when I gave them my heart-felt plea?

What if my requests for federal authorities had been taken seriously, forcing the dirty 5-0 and the Pelicans to leave me alone?

Maybe then, I wouldn't feel like a jailbird fugitive, too terrified to ever step foot back in Monterey—or even California—out of fear of these f*ckin' Pelicans and corrupt fuzz.

What if the Monterey Police escalated their phony narrative to cover their own tracks, telling those close to me that there were no suspects to investigate, and no threats reported just to orchestrate my arrest?

What if back at the police station, the 'higher-ups' uncovered the beat-cop body cameras recording me asking where a certain officer was that day, and that they replied: *"It's his day off."*

Then I said, *"So... he is the one that shined a red sniper light on my chest, across the street at the Navy lawyers then?"*

The moment those words left my mouth, the police abruptly bee-lined out of the house, but not before the Officers told the person closest to me that I was not a threat to myself or anyone else.

What if—since I said that officer's name on camera—the state-sponsored criminals used my family to stage a gavel-and-gag, fake federal marshal routine, arresting me while working overtime to get me 5150'd?

What if the Sheriff who escorted me into the Monterey County jail in Salinas got caught videotaping me while getting undressed during the intake process from her body cam? (August 31, 2023)

What if jail sheriffs reportedly don't wear body cams on their uniforms—only cameras on the walls, which don't cover the dressing area. Yet there she was, standing directly in front of me, just a couple of feet away, her camera on as she verbally accosted me with three iterations: *"Bend over more! Spread wider! Cough harder!"*—repeated three times.

What if Monterey County Jail were in contempt, and state or federal funding was stripped due to their inhumane cell conditions, and degrading treatment that was never rectified while under federal supervision from the *Hernandez* case?

Protective custody cells reeking of piss and shit, with remnants smeared throughout.

Sinks corroded and spewing discolored water so metallic and foul-smelling it was undrinkable—yet I had to choke it down out of sheer desperation since staff denied any other option.

What if this putrid water spiked my blood pressure to dangerous levels, leaving me on nurse-watch, verge of heart attack?

What if I spent seven days in protective custody since the Monterey Police never submitted the bogus charges to the court because they knew I was innocent, and they feared having me on a court record explaining the horrific crucibles they collectively put me through?

What if the temporary dissociative breakdown I had after leaving Monterey when everything hit me at once—will one day be an event I can teach others about—rather than something that consumes my life and cripples me into hibernation?

What if I did not flee California with only a backpack leaving my whole life behind? What if two years later, I am still aching through somatic pains and post-traumatic stress-like symptoms?

What if the Cankered-Blue-Iniquitous of Monterey were anchored in liability for their illegal activity?

241

✿ The following comes straight from my experience as a customer. My qualms are on record—not that it mattered. They brushed me off and parroted, *"That's not possible."*

What if Apple uses 'dog doors' in its systems enabling segmented access to high-level hackers—ahem, the government— to 'break into,' whilst both Norton and Lookout installed, rendering their software a useless waste of money?

What if Jeffrey Epstein pictures don't magically appear as app icons, and Chase bank phone calls don't casually reroute themselves to some woman threatening me to check my brakes?

Let's not even talk about the gross edits and vanishing acts performed on my Adobe InDesign files.

What if Norton or Lookout had the balls to stand up for their customers and call out Apple for those dog doors, especially since their software clearly failed to protect me?

Oh wait, can it be true? Does Norton and

Lookout provide dog doors per compelled compliance?

What if Lookout refused to acknowledge my account because confessing that their software failed would have jeopardized the $223 million-dollar sale to F-Secure, along with other investor news released shortly after I contacted them?

Emailed customer service on January 9, 2023 @ 4:03 PM. Then, January 22, 2023 @ 6:09 AM—press@lookout.com.

Real smooth Lookout—you got that partnership with Verizon.

What if Lookout and Norton didn't want the world to know their software is nothing more than an expensive hallucination?

What if these Fourth Amendment violations are on the—it's on a gag-order basis—and if you are not being gagged, you don't need to know?

What if F-Secure has no clue that the software they purchased from Lookout is a piece-of-shit?

Or worse—what if F-Secure knows that the software is a piece-of-shit because of the dog-doored compelled compliance, but bought it anyway knowing it's a cash-cow?

After all, consumers are often in a blissful illusion of safety, trusting corporate and government assurances, while remaining unaware of the deep vulnerabilities embedded within the very services we purchase.

What if this is only attainable due to government bestowed secrecy mandates—wielded to shield all involved, including the private sector from accountability—since their products and services defraud and deceive in pursuit of intelligence without warrants to maximize profits, and elevate stock portfolios?

What if Apple tells porkies to the public, splitting-hairs-with-words, claiming no 'backdoors,' giving segmented access and are L O O S E Y - G O O S E Y with their lack-of-privacy... parts?

What if the dirty government piggies that I crossed don't need warrants, while the common hackers don't make the cut. What if Norton and Lookout will happily notify you about the low-level hackers?

But, when it's the colonial scams of Uncle Sam's, and their spawns that are Star-Spangled-Filth—radio silence since they are *'legally'* shielded from **any** recourse.

Challenging these illegalities is within the stated missions of the EFF, ACLU, CCR, and Amnesty. To me, their legal advocacy looks more like pageantry for notoriety.

Million-Dollar-Question: Are these—civil rights advocacies—a smoke screen meant to make us *widdle* Americans believe they actually give a poo-poo?

Oh, the irony—if my pro se filing helps ensure warrants are obtained before invading the privacy of Americans.

What if the government is fraudulently applying gag orders as a catch-all weapon, so they can do whatever they want?

Meanwhile, I am sitting here betting my life that they are: Contravening, disobeying, infringing, transgressing, encroaching upon, breaching, impinging on, subverting, perverting, and ultimately profaning the Constitution and the backbone of the United States.

FISA gag orders are deeply problematic since they're indefinite, offer no sunset or review mechanism to provide individualized justification, while suppressing criticism rather than protecting American's privacy and our God-Given-Rights.

Baring companies from notifying users or the public, while often providing no realistic process for challenging their legality, creating a structure of secrecy that resists accountability with federal laws.

What if Apple doubles down on its lied effort and calls out Norton, Lookout, and F-Secure by publicly committing that their security software is as *risk-free* as posting your home address on social media while broadcasting that you're on vacation—and that you're leaving your front door unlocked, inviting squatters to swing by, whip up a sammie, and take over your life?

Or better yet—using *password* as your password?

What if the employees at Seaside FedEx had not taken orders from the Pelicans to remove my plea-for-life letters—all of which required signatures upon arrival?

What if they were addressed to the CEOs of AT&T, Google, Apple, Lookout, Norton, X, as well as the White House and Tucker Carlson & Brett Baer at FOX News—crucial in exposing the truth and seeking justice?

Cameras and tracking numbers don't lie:
391176808426, 391176856851,
391176961680, 391177037243,
391177089891, 391177148655,
391177211352, 391177286843.

John Hancocks were required, but it never reached its intended audience. What if they had? What if those letters sparked the action I needed to save my life?

What if FedEx CEO Raj Subramaniam, his EA—or whoever signed for it—read the letter I sent regarding Seaside FedEx and chose to do the noble thing?

What if these Grim Reapers of Correspondence were slapped on the hand for raiding my Hail-Mary's?

Tracking #393762699211; follow-up email to abuse@fedex.com on February 10, 2023, @ 10:48 AM PT.

Those do-or-die memos, painstakingly written, printed, and sealed right in front of the young associate—with the manager looming over trying to read what I wrote—somehow arrived at the intended destinations completely unoccupied of ink.

How does a letter written at, printed, signed and stuffed by me end up blank upon delivery?

Per tracking history, a second label was created for a new envelope after I left with a lighter weight. FedEx sent one or no pages—

my letter was two tree-skins, stapled.

What if Norton's Escalation Team confirmed via email that it came empty and the proof of signature was an employee on January 20, 2023 @ 1:36 PM?

What if this coordinated campaign to silence my cry for justice is far more concerning, and I opened a huge can of deceit?

In April 2022, the Foreign Intelligence Surveillance Court ("FISC") audited the intelligence agencies, but only called out one single FBI field office for their over 278,000 unlawful searches of US persons.

What if FISC published the full scroll of how many ghosts lurked within the FBI, NSA and CIA—and definitively stated *"this many queries crossed the line"* with the respective, not-to-be-confused-with-respected— intelligence agencies?

What if the CIA, NSA, FBI and others, including the private sector companies who allow segmented access—think Google,

Apple, ChatGPT, Xfinity, META—peep-in whenever they get their penises tickled and are bored—as they help the ticklers for retaliation and revenge?

What if our government is hiding more, because if we really knew what was going on since we out number them—all dem-duckers would be... in serious twouble per poetic, street justice through *due process*?

What if warrants were only necessary to present evidence in court, but not required to spy on innocent people for the amusement of power-hungry, deviated minds who pull the strings behind closed doors?

What if this unchecked surveillance was not about protecting national security, but about enabling a sinister circle of insiders to gather dirt and silence anyone who might rip the blinders off their corruption, while they smugly laugh in their gilded echo chambers?

What if Attorney General Bondi, Director Patel and Deputy Director Bongino rebuked these agents, officers, and private parties for treating the U.S. Constitution, human decency, and civil rights like some expensive private boarding school with $100K a-year tuition—where federal and state laws are optional and don't apply to them... not yet or maybe never?

When does the government enforce the laws on themselves?

Then again... what if this surveillance-heavy, 'nursing, teaching and more are no longer professional degrees' idea is part of the Handmaid's Tale of a new world order?

It's terrifying what bureaucratic creeps can do with high-grade tech and low-grade morals. While the state-fed lapdogs cheer with Sticks, soaking in their crook-fest at Stillwaters—17-miles of crocodile smiles— as the Pelicans tee-off after their all-they-can-deplete, Monique.

What if the FBI and DOJ leadership respected the Constitution more than internal politics—I mean, what if my little stand-up for our rights, force whomever is serving the Vipers and someone in power finally does the noble thing?

An American Citizen can dream that she actually lives in the 'Land of the Free.'

What if the DOJ does the honorable thing and investigates the dirty Monterey Police and Pelicans?

What if white-hat hackers uncover the lead Pelican, linking him to his father's shady history with payphones that are conveniently scrubbed from the company website to hide any breadcrumbs?

What if these hackers with integrity also unveil the lead Pelican's company who participates in surveillance through his 'communications' company and clients?

What if the so-called, sought-out destination was not merely a picturesque retreat, but a covert surveillance hub— its conference rooms and luxury rentals wired to harvest words never meant for their ears?

What if there are blackmail plots and insider trading schemes hatched from intel stolen during private, corporate meetings, while the unsuspecting elite sipped their overpriced cocktails?

What if Xfinity boasts about their report abuse process on their website, but their lack of help says they could care less since they got paid and are part of the problem?

What if real estate agents and brokers have a property listed at $5.5 million, but secretly come across a buyer offering $500k cash under the table?

What if, to the public, they drop the price on the MLS to $5 million—while keeping the sticker-price behind closed doors at $5.5— unreported to the IRS?

What if they pocket the cash for their own gain, while simultaneously driving down the neighborhood's property value, screwing over everyone involved, including their business partner—smugly blaming the market—a seller's jackpot at the time?

What if this little book takes flight, igniting a movement among justice-driven truth-seekers?

What if those so often dismissed as 'conspiracy theorists,' rally behind me en masse?

What if our collective power impels a reckoning from the Pelicans, their lemmings, the Poisoned Peelers, and those sham companies for their false promises of security, egregious abuses of power, vengeful harassment, and insidious lies?

What if, after all this, I suddenly woke up to bask in the revelation that my life was nothing more than an ongoing nightmare— a long, dark corridor of chaos—only to emerge into the fantasized and idolized life I have always prayed for?

Murder. Suicide. Silence.

"Ding, ding, ding!"

The not-so-subtle, utterly grating sound of a spoon clanking against the side of a coffee cup, startled me on command as it instantly flooded my all with the heebie-jeebies.

"I need some coffee, Monique. Pause your game and get up—right now!" Pops barked from the kitchen.

For those who are blissfully unaware, this was an old-school patriarchal tradition when someone would bang a utensil against a cup to summon the wife, child, or unlucky servant to refill a drink.

Wipe the idea of a riveting conversation being interrupted—except, no one else was in the room.

Father sat alone at the kitchen table, mere steps from the coffee pot. I, on the other hand, was three times farther away in the living room minding my own business.

As always, I leaped into action. Grabbed his precious mug and refilled it to avoid any misunderstandings.

Setting the freshly brewed, high-octane morning nectar down beside him, Pops casually asked, *"You know I had a brother, right?"*

"Yes, I know a little about Uncle Gary, but you never told me what happened to him." I said, all twelve years old and teetering on the edge of a truth I was not sure I wanted to hear.

Daddio did not look up. His head dipped lower as his pen wandered across the yellow notepad, doodling random sketches of some indigenous or tribal figure—along with his signature—over and over, again.

An oppressive murmur of grief and avoidance, hung-heavy in the air between us. Dad's aversion to meet my gaze when talking about his family was painfully familiar. It was the kind of silence where your body trembled for another word, standing unsure whether you were obliged to leave.

It was like looking me in the eye might crack open the floodgates of an emotion he didn't dare validate. That would have made it all too real, something he could not—would not—cope with.

Instead, the Old Man let the truth about his family and himself corrode in some dark corner of his mind, safely out of reach.

Let's dig into the why—why couldn't he have been the kind of father who healed and loved, instead of hurt?

And the most pressing question... Could Pops have been as capable as his brother?

According to the family written obituary, Grandpa Sam Arge was born in 1919 in the United States. In his early years, he worked tirelessly on the railroads and in the coal mines of Utah—grueling labor that fueled his tough-as-nails demeanor.

At twenty-two, just after the attack on

Pearl Harbor, Gramps answered the call to serve, enlisting in the Army Air Corps.

During World War II, he participated in North Africa, the Liberation of Italy, and took part in the invasion of Europe.

When he returned home, he bore the marks of his service with pride, having earned *'thirteen'* battle stars.

The original family name is Greek—it was either Argyros or Argyropoulos—shortened to Arge along the way.

This peculiar change comes with its own mystery. Who did it—and why—remains unclear. There's no way I am reaching out to Dad's close family members for numerous reasons.

One, I don't want to impede upon my current path or risk dislodging the very thing driving me to pursue my goal of becoming a writer.

The other... well, broken family *stuff.*

If they came through Ellis Island, maybe

'Arge' was just a simplified version to avoid confusion.

But then, there's a part of me that chokes on the idea that there might be a darker reason behind the change.

We-shall-see.

At some point after Gramps returned, Father was born on April 11, 1946.

As the firstborn, he saddled up with the responsibility for everything and everyone— no exceptions. It was irrelevant about what went wrong or who was to blame—he was the bearer of fault.

Pops fired off how Gramps gave him serious ass-whoopings. There were at least two beatings that were so atrocious that he ended up in the hospital.

When Dad reiterated that he was the only one hit, I gave him a hard stare—my frown silently screamed, *"Are you really ignoring the elephant in the room, typing on a laptop?"* By then he was plenty generous with the whips handed to me.

At any rate, the Old Man soldiered on as he explained how Gramps had skyscraper high expectations. Impossible standards at home and at school, with every set of instructions. When Dad did not deliver, it was straight-up unrelenting affliction, pure and simple.

The fact that Pops never spoke about Gary left me with little to go on. Perchance, watching Dad endure those drastic beatings or whatever Gary witnessed, combined with his own life landmines scattered across the terrain, must have been enough to shape his own struggles.

Bound by these blood-esque relationships with Dad's family, most of what I know is based on fragments and assumptions, sprinkled with the few details Pops reluctantly articulated. It was not until I was about eighteen that I ferreted out our family's darkest secret—or at least, what I assume is the darkest.

But with this clan, who knows?

Nothing else comes to mind that could top this level of malevolence—no question. It's a stain so deep and unprincipled, it leaves a slim chance for admittance to the Pearly Gates.

Who knows whether any amount of repentance, or 180-degree effort to turn one's life around—had he survived—could have cleansed this act enough for eternity with the Almighty Himself.

Why? Well, because it was not a mistake, nor was it done in self-defense. It was calculated and premeditated.

It took writing these chaotic breaths and delving into this hush-hush horror for me to theorize why I was met with a sudden cold shoulder when school resumed after summer break in 1991—entering fourth grade.

I slowly began to piece together why the friends I once shared sleepovers and laughter with suddenly treated like I carried some kind of contagious, deadly disease.

Around eight years old, I was blissfully

unaware of the difference between heartache that stings internally—to betrayals that devastate your world, leaving you with only one option: to dissect your purpose and shed the dead weight that held you back.

When I approached my fellow munchkins to say hello, they would scatter like startled pigeons, as if they didn't even know me. No more hanging out on the playground, no more walking to class together.

My once close circle was reduced to a distant crowd of silent breaths of muffled whispers—caught giggling behind cupped hands with mocked laughter as my pony tail quickly swung back in forth when I walked. The mystery of this behavior chipped away at my spirit, leaving me questioning what was wrong with me.

So, what sparked this sudden, *"I have cooties... stay away attitude toward me?"*

Well, Gary was some type of developer or general contractor with two partners for a land development project or something in that realm.

On June 24, 1991, at Bernstein Realty in San Francisco—during what I infer must have been the final round of financing for this deal—a business meeting took an inexplicable turn.

One article reported that Gary was found on the floor, with two revolvers by his side and a bullet through his chest.

His two business partners were also dead, yet the specific location of their wounds went unmentioned—a detail that was at best, selective—and at worst, suspicious.

All I managed to uncover in an article was that *"they believed"* Gary to be the named shooter and the one who committed suicide.

That's where the plot thickens for me... or unravels, depending on your outlook.

Why would Gary have two revolvers and a gunshot in his chest? Where were the gunshots on the other victims? Isn't it a bit cumbersome to hide two guns in business suit or tight clothes back then?

How do you get past the secretary who was reported to be there with those weapons?

What is more astonishing is the article I found in *The Noe Valley Voice,* written by Denise Minor.

Apparently the Bernstein family had enough pull not only to secure the front page, but enough leeway for a short story—perfect for a *clear-headed* grieving widow to get her... story—out.

It was noted: *"she wanted to talk to the Noe Valley Voice in order to set the record straight about the events surrounding her husband's murder."*

Bernstein's widow: *"I haven't been able to bring myself to read the news accounts. But from what I have heard, there have been some inaccuracies printed, and I want the truth to be told."*

All of the articles that I found were negative against Gary.... Interesting.

Historically speaking—husbands tell their wifes the hundred-percent truth in every situation and never skew the facts to make themselves look better, right?

No man has *ever* lied and withheld a gambling debt or business deal they fubbed.

Everyone basically implied that Gary planned some wild-west showdown, dual wielding pistols like an outlaw. The visual itself feels absurd.

Curious and unsatisfied me sent a digital request to the police station to learn more.

Their response?

The incident was *"too long ago"* to provide any further details.

Well... obviously—but at least I tried.

What threw me off was when I told one of the Pelicans that I was adding a new angle to my book—doubting that Gary committed suicide—he was adamant that I shouldn't include that perspective. He insisted that it was—according to him—a suicide.

Why would this Pelican push me not to write it? What was it to him?

To be fair, that's exactly the kind of details the FBI or CIA would have had insight into. *Especially given who...*

My longish arms can reach, but... noting how uncommon my last name is, I wager the Pelicans had this horrid day on their radar by 2019—when they did a deep dive in my life for the NDA situation—before I decided to write this part in 2022.

Let's cut to the chase—self-inflicted gunshot with a revolver to the chest?

I. Just. Can't.

The curiosity crusader in me mentally paces like a salesperson strung out on coke—was one revolver planted? Because having two guns by Gary remains a mystery to me.

Let me be crystal clear: I am confident Gary fatally harmed at least one person or both that day.

But there is a fire in my gut that won't let me shake the feeling that a bandit—someone aligned with the two business partners was in the room.

Perhaps this mysterious figure inflicted the fatal chest wound on Gary after he shot the two business partners. Then left his revolver beside Gary to stage the scene, slipping out of a bustling downtown building unnoticed, avoiding suspicion amid the uproar of gunfire.

Alternatively, Gary may of have had a sidekick who pulled the trigger at one of the partners, then fled, leaving the gun by Gary to avoid being caught with it. However, that wouldn't explain Gary's wound.

Unless there were five people there—two against three—and two escaped, one from each side.

The more I think about it, the more the threads unravel into a snarl of possibilities.

Most inexplicably—if Gary's sidekick did exist, a darker and far more unsettling question creeps in: Could it have been my father?

From what I have pieced together, they were close. But the Old Man—well, when all is said and done, he never wanted to talk about *that* day.

This makes my stomach want to heave from the probable conjecture that refuses to fade. Of course, this is all inference. The truth was lost in the fog of time, buried with those who knew it best.

I hate to say this—huge, colossal gasp—how did those around Gary miss-the-signs?

Drifting in the undercurrents of my think-quatic, waves of thoughts had me wonder when others saw the name 'Arge'—were they instantly drowned in the deep swells of shock? Gagging and asphyxiating on this devastating loss that rippled through families, friends, and the local community?

Viewpoints will always reshape the story.

Spinning the wheel the other way—if I had a child, and their friend's uncle was plastered all over the local news for a travesty like this, I would have done the same.

I can see why those parents told their

kids to steer clear of me—if that's why I had cooties anyway. Maybe I was already f*cked up by then?

Growing up, our family missed the mark on a pivotal life lesson—the importance of seeking help when you feel trapped with no way out—and the hard truth that fiery tempers run deep in the father's side of the bloodline.

Conversations could have centered on recognizing when you're overwhelmed, reaching out for guidance when you're lost, and embracing vulnerability as a sign of bravery—not weakness. Allowing your imperfect flaws to be seen is where real intrepidity begins.

Gary's pride, I presume, drained his emotional reservoir dry, convincing himself that he couldn't weather financial or public failure. In the end, he and possibly they, chose the unthinkable, worst case scenario—stealing the lives, love, healing and new beginnings from both families.

No matter how hollow the hour, or how fierce the crisis of faith, it's never too late to rise from the ashes—to reimagine, to rebuild, and to create an elevated life that is enriched with extraordinary and limitless possibilities.

Reassessing the early chapters of life, I learned a stark truth: unchecked ego is often the silent saboteur. It clouds judgment, fuels irrational conduct as it blinds respectful and ethical solutions.

Pride and ego spin a fantasy of power—an eroding web of self-perception, glistening and delicate, yet doomed to tear at the first harsh wind or rash touch.

Arrogance and narcissism create a barrier that values appearances over authenticity—it slams the door shut on those offering a hand, as if they're strangers lurking in the dark.

But here's the real power—accepting and owning when you have hit rock-bottom. And yes, even if your lowest-of-lows, reveals a basement below it. Hold no disgrace in taking the high road to start anew.

The weight of Gary's actions leaves a trembling dimness that words can scarcely describe. No matter how much shame and sorrow I feel for the harm caused, I will never be able to rewrite the past or erase its consequences.

What I can do, though, is decide where my energy goes from here, and I intently choose to pour it into something meaningful.

By sharing my journey, scars, and truths, I aim to rekindle the sleeping flame in others.

To prove that even in the bleakest void of uncertainty, in the strangled depths of despair—when you think or feel that there's no one left to turn to—remember that a glimmer of light still exists: a resurrection of life will arise, when you're polished-by-pain.

Once you turn, pain-into-purpose.

May my act of vulnerability be someone else's first step toward healing. Just as sharing it has been undeniably metamorphic for me.

unraveling

Falling low,
and hard,
is truly a beautiful gift.

New appreciation for what you have,
for what you might have lost,
no matter the cost,
or the lines that were crossed.

This is a tender restart,
for your beating heart.

A final chance,
to make things right.

To work on what is broken.

Fight for what you love.

Live every moment to the fullest,
with faith for another tomorrow.

polished-by-pain

Passionately persevering through pain,
purposefully.

Pinpoint progress over perfection.

Pursue procured potential,
by promising your psyche
to practice patience
while progressing with poise,
precision,
and persistent probity.

Purified perspectives prepare,
and promote the pursuit,
to prevail through pitfalls
and predicaments.

Polishing possibilities on pathways,
procuring a profound peace,
and prosperity,
with peak pliability.

Unsolicited
Advice

Five minutes ago I was your Queen,
you were my King.

Your actions self-professed
thirty folds of betrayal.

This time delay has no endgame,
blitzing you desperado.

They call me the underrated Grandmaster
that captured your blunders
from down under.

I am the Back-Rank-Mate.
Your fatal surprise that tells no lies.

My self-discovery laughs
at your random wood-pushing.
Refrain from your tragic remains,
I mock your novice game.

Open file and save our past, Mr. Fools Mate.
Time for you to hang
with your poisoned pawns.

Forfeited any chance to touch my pieces,
you are out of moves with me.

Go on now... flee, *flea*.
I stopped you from biting me.

It didn't matter anyhow,
your tempo never materialized
to anything meaningful.

Your active piece, is not an absolute pin.

This automation game you play,
is made for blind pigs that know no better.

Clock move this Stalemate,
I crushed you before
you could see it coming.

This ain't no dead... draw.
Deflecting you so hard,
you were stabbed like a skewer.

The sudden death of us,
brings past due life to me now.

This is Checkmate Boy...
See, I am not your toy.
Although I wish you the best,
it's time you lay down to rest.

Karma Will Be There For You

Perfectly imperfect because
perfection does not exist.

Vicious cycles for appearance,
appears lost in meaning.

Diminishing others' self-worth,
from fabricated tea that is spread,
opens a torrent straight to hate's head,
enticing bloodshed.

With that said, time to mandate their fate,
as I bait and berate,
those who don't play straight,
in my home state.

No more chasing tails of dogs
that bite my back,
just left me gasping for breath...
false panic attack.

Save those crocodile smiles and baby tears.
This fake drama melody,
leaves karma as the remedy.

Who Am I?

Overthinking,
I have no feeling.

Only stray thoughts,
with lost words.

This all paved my rocky road.

Eyes are open,
mind is engaged,
with a heart free to love.

I can finally breathe naturally.

Bright lights,
and shiny stars,
I am ready for you to find me.

I hope,
we will never...
let go.

Tired of My... Own Shit!

My ego acted like a lunatic by repeatedly lying to myself that my upbringing didn't obliterate my cognitive architecture. That if I presented myself as *put together* and stable without interrogating my unwitting mirage—somehow—I would be labeled as *normal.*

Instead, my attention was commandeered by the masses, projecting my speculations onto their areas of need—which, frankly, was none of my beeswax.

I had no right to use my transference services in other people's supersaturated beehives, whether I detected that they needed assistance or not.

These misguided, servant-hearted aids?

Had me living a stuck-in-a-pickle life, making me lose my crunch as I became immersed in mold—squishy, soft, and over delicate. Only for me to break apart when salvaged by users who washed and cleaned me up for others that were starving.

It wasn't until Dad perished that I tasted the acrimonious truth. Even though I was walking around—light as a feather—I still was distraught by my fluctuating emotions.

Despite being grateful that our tug-of-war was decisively over, I clashed with regret—a yearning for the forgiveness we both wished upon a star for, but we let our pride block us at every turn.

If only we had silenced our egos and listened to the ache in our hearts, I would not have mournful bouts periodically when he popped up in my mind. The upside of this downside was, I started to act like I was a priority. That I was—am—worthy.

For the first time, I saw myself as an actual, breathing—human—who was alive on earth, as my mind overflowed with everything I longed to accomplish. It dawned on me that I was neither too young nor too old, that I still had a decent stretch of years ahead.

With this newfound resolve to bloom-from-decay, all I had were questions: How do I use this precious time for a meaningful impact? How do I arm myself with these costly lessons and transform them into wisdom?

Not to mention, I have the zeal and prowess to live—The American Dream.

Reinvigorated by a brief reprieve from the furnace of affliction, I ached for a moment I could be alone. The renewed energy surging through me awakened a hidden facet of my being—one that thrilled me breathlessly with exhilaration.

I stood on the cusp of stripping my soul bare, probing what truly enamored me—deciphering the solutions to my mental complexities while turning my aspirations into reality.

Within me, a lifetime of utterances gathered in a synaptic storm, begging to be uncaged. Yet, I couldn't shake the guilt of feeling selfish for wanting to put my needs first. I began this journey a day or so after the Old Man passed, so the craved me-time was on hold until I could be tagged out of my grieving *responsibilities.*

Now on the mend, I intend to transcend my writing by igniting these desires with amplifiers.

Slinging text all willy-nilly has always been my tranquilly state of mind, even if I was wholly misaligned, leaving me to be unkind to my behind.

As I approach the halfway mark of my expiry date, it's finally time to create, to reinstate my fate, regardless of the self-doubt that always left me sketched-out.

The 'Holy Grail of Word Domination' that is thundering through my brain has me point-blank captivated, and gloriously restless on this new quest to cure myself.

These reveries were about to explode like an erratic driver slamming into a fire hydrant—water spewing straight up into the air.

To kick off my 'wordipulator' endeavor, I was overdue for a trip to the stationary store. This fever of an unmet need had my desires burning for a well-crafted journal and a bold, fancy pen worthy of blessing the colossal undertaking I was about to embark on.

Even though I had no clear visualization of which life ordeal I would tackle first to get to the nitty-gritty of my cognitive malfunctions—there was a flowing sense that this was about to be a turbulent adventure for me.

It had been about fifteen years since I tried writing anything personal—poems, musings, or what have you. Ideas always drifted around in my inner-workings, but they never seemed to swim ashore and land on a coherent train-of-thought.

Overly excited to start jotting lines down, I had one indispensable stop I needed to make first. My liver begged me to reconsider, but my derelict conditioning screamed,

"*F*ck yes!*" to rag water. Because, let's face it—I was about to excavate mummies.

Uncertain how long this bender would last, I made sure to position myself so that, when the craving struck, I could fill the chalice of want.

At a warehouse-style store, I ended up buying not just the booze I initially planned on, but an indulgent selection of extras. Each bottle tantalized my taste buds as they looked sinfully luscious in these stupendous amounts.

It looked as though I was preparing for a party with a cohort of rascals, but nope— just *me*.

While loading the trunk of my car, I got overly stoked for this self-help work party for one. I was more than ready to kick this shindig off without a hitch.

The ancient, long-lost ruins and ancestral curses that were wrapped in rot and buried within me, could not wait one more second.

Animatedly, I swooped up my journal and arranged it beneath my right arm, with a liquor concoction balanced in my left finger bones. Heading towards Pops' oversized pixel flatty, I slumped onto the couch, ready to just... *be.*

That moment turned out to be wildly penetrating for me. I guzzled my liquid encouragement, slurping it down like a 7-11 slushie on a sweltering, hundred-eleven degree day.

In unison with the shadow of mind's door, I was already contemplating the next round before the ice in my glass had a chance to melt. The pint was never on the coffee table for an extended period of time to leave a single ring of condensation behind.

My untouched journal, paired with its elegant pen, sat anxiously to my right— primed for that quick, on-the-draw reflex, when the long-overdue time struck. Even then, I remained fixated on conquering drink three. Which, for the lightweights out there equates to about eight.

Time to wait patiently for my nervous system to sync up with thy brain, to align with thy body, anticipating that peak moment of numbing... *perfection.*

It was then, and only then, that I knew it was time to face my scarring music and to put my writing tools to restorative, clever use.

Once I started writing... I could. Not. Stop.

Whether it was alcohol or a lifetime of suppressed emotions collapsing through the floodgates, it all poured out from my hands.

An unstoppable surge—not unlike the high probability that dirties in our government, and their quid pro quo allies in the lithium or quartz business, are guiding storms through cloud seeding with perfected artificial weather modification techniques—rumored to have been in development since the 1940s.

Dam-tampering... man-made hurricane.

I-mean-crane—look at that crane!

Birds are so majestical.

It was like my liberation—my very life—depended on these scribbles, while none of it registered in my brain. Almost as though my soul had floated out of my body, leaving me as nothing more than an onlooker soaking it all in.

On no occasion did I ever deduce this magnified level of ambition was plausible. There's no way I can adequately explain what I was experiencing—defying anything I had ever felt before.

Doing my best to paint this picture for you, all I can say is that the depth of my being vocalized its needs.

It was my inner child who pined for love, peace, and closure. My little nipper who was never given a chance, was having the last word.

The dark side of me was hypnotized by the light, drawing me toward an inner-essence expedition that led me down the painful path to revivification—a metamorphosis of purification and transcendence.

During this self-cultivation, I had a revelation: writing was the only 'round-of-drugs' on the market, including black, with the efficacy to redeem my heart, mind, body, and soul.

By the next morning, reality had a different game plan—the ever-so-fun scenario of hangover guilt.

The ole' few steps forward, to a jump, and fallin' on my ass—back.

This here body fully surrendered from the previous nights' dereliction of gulping down those adult bevies. It was almost as if I were sleepwalking, trying to recall anything verbatim I had cooked-up in my diary.

Making a beeline to the kitchen, I brewed an ultra-strong cup of coffee. After a few gulps, a semblance of normalcy returned as I regained control of my senses.

The caffeine was kicking thy basal forebrain, and turbo charging my mental synthesis like Bruce Lee launching Bob Wall in Enter the Dragon.

I scrambled to gather myself as I braced for the raw truths that I had scribbled down. It was time to put my feet up and stabilize myself for what I was about to uncover— a deep-dive into the chaos of my mind, when alcohol had complete control over me.

Only for an immediate hemorrhage of remorse to follow as I screamed aloud, *"Holy shit! What the absolute f*ck?"*

Everything pointed to now, but all I could do was close my journal and go about my day as if I hadn't read the disturbing syllables breaking my orbit—let alone that I was the one who wrote them.

I was for reals shocked at the excruciating distress laid bare in those words.

These fancy materials were stowed away for the time being. I was not remotely ready to face all that pain-I-felt-inside—especially now that it was glaringly obvious that my roots were blighted and declining in health at an unbecoming rate.

Yet, there was a flicker-of-relief, having

glimpsed the veracity that framed my life's quandary.

With a hunch of the strenuous road ahead, it became clear there would be no turning back after this. Eventually I would be irrevocably ready to face the misleading reality I had depicted.

But... not anytime soon.

Lost in a vicious cycle of heavy drinking and blind writing, I poured my heart out, anxiously awaiting a response from my mind—but it was not made up yet.

Abandoned by my cognitive odyssey thanks to this damaged heart of mine, I was too scared to review those words until at least five months had passed.

In the meantime, I kept on truckin' with my writing and no reviewing. My scribblings fluctuated between inspirational poetry, to garbage-of-the-mouth feelings, with no other emotions in-between.

Once curiosity got the best of me, the tide

turned to call my own number and break this unrelenting cycle of nothingness. At last, I was ready to pay-the-piper.

Bracing myself, I clawed my nails into my skin, and ripped the masking tape off my eyelids, leaving no eyebrows behind.

It was beyond time to put unwavering efforts toward self-love and resolving my issues, as I could not afford any more tissues. Since I was done choking my life away, it was time to figure out how to work through the unworked.

I marveled at how much of my life was spent faking it till I made it—only I had been faking it far more than I had ever made it. Slowly, I sluggishly began to comprehend how degraded I was on the inside, only to be amazed by how well I managed to cover it up.

As if my internal components had suffered a shotgun blow that scattered me into a million-little-pieces. The only thing I was capable of was haphazardly slapping my innards back together unevenly with Scotch tape.

Bits and pieces of my overlooked parts dangled and flapped around in the wrong vicinity since they were not good enough for a second glance over to be put back where they belonged.

Whenever I ingested anything or even sneezed, fragments of me would release since the adhesive denied being bonded with my never-ending, do-nothing-to-better-myself, pity-party.

I no longer had the mental reserves to keep this 'long-con' going. Looking back on my accomplishments—or lack thereof—created the perfect breeding ground for unbridled, decadent-detours to take hold.

Almost like spoiled milk that is still newly sealed in its gallon container, simmering on a sidewalk under Jacobabad's noon-sun.

Bacteria fermenting within the lactose, creating carbon dioxide and lactic acid. A mucked-up, stagnant-self leaking sour milk—a fizzing, fetid rupture-of-decay born from false preservation and stagnant repression.

The person I was fifteen years ago, was almost identical to who I was in that second. There were no fresh spools of thought—just the same moth-filled corpses, mis-mashing in dusty old cobwebs that were echoing in an abandoned mindset.

The only thing I was consistent at was getting older and a slightly slim-pickin' wiser from the perpetual list of mistakes that I executed *correctly*—only to be quickly forgot about so I could repeat history for shits-and-giggles.

Living this life like a chameleon trying to adapt to my environment as if I knew what I was doing and belonged, had me break my tail off more times than was known to be possible.

At this point of convergence—where serenity's clock struck zero—every road guided me toward uncovering what was truly within or was it merely something I had seen in others and chose to embody?

To get to my rallying point, it was time to

create my baseline self, or a clean canvas if you will.

The spirit-excavation plan was easy to devise, but reprogramming my streamlet of awareness was another story. It proved to be a mix of death-defying roller coasters and bandwagons I eagerly mounted, only to go arse over apex and hit the ground like a sack of potatoes, more times than necessary.

My mind was like a mentally explosive boxing match, comparable to the infamous '97 fight with the world's most intimidating boxer—Mike Tyson—*nibble-nibble.*

The next moment, I would devolve into a scripted [?] pansy nothingness:

P a u l - E - W a n t - a - C r a c k e r ?

Totally f*cked to un-f*cked process, so to say.

Any sane person would have gotten the hint, but I liked to reconfirm the confirmed, already approved basic knowledge on what not-to-do, when no-you-shouldn't was already established.

One thing about me with an extremist personality type that needs to feel diverse levels of everything—always in for a wild ride in one way or another.

Eventually, my heart-fire persistence not to abuse myself anymore won me a second chance in this life—propelling me forward to work on positioning my addictive personality in an advantageous way.

My first initiative was to seek out self-care books, in the hopes to reprogram my inner monologue with encouraging words of wisdom.

As it turned out, those mental health books were way too fake and fluffy-soft for me to relate to. There were no words strung together in a way I could connect with. To me, it was like they were written by people who had never undergone high-level trauma.

Not only did I feel completely defeated after diving into these books, but it was also humiliating to learn how emotionally stunted I was at such a young age—I couldn't even grasp the basics. 294

I barely made it twenty pages into each before giving up as I ruminated, *"Wow, I am seriously messed up. Is this how normal, healthy people think all the time? I am so f*cked."*

On the hunt for motivational material that was edgy—something with the power to plant a seed and awaken a thriving brain—one that could turn my mind-shavings into feeling gleefully enthusiastic.

Clearly, raw and edgy is not how these books are authored to work. Nevertheless, I managed to extract a few takeaways for my psychotherapeutic voyage, even if the journey wasn't quite what I expected.

I first adopted a chipper, nothing-will-bother-me attitude to cultivate a naturally positive mindset. My subconscious deduced that I needed to be on the opposite end of the spectrum from negativity to meet my dream self somewhere in the middle.

Time to immerse myself on the bright side of everything—24/7.

Being ecstatic every second of the day was at the forefront of my thought-bucket. It was time to be pleased with the whole-kit-and-caboodle. Whenever I faltered in jocundity, I replayed the following to recalibrate my life compass:

"Someone has it worse off. I have running water, a roof over my head, good health—to the best of my knowledge—food on the table, shoes on thy feet, and my beloved motorcycle."

I didn't allow myself—or anyone close to me—to express anything but a full-on zest for it all, with everything in between.

Each time others' feelings arose, I would counter them with examples of why we should be content—to stay grounded in the bright side and never indulge in negativity or ingratitude.

To harness that inner happiness you feel as a kid—eating cotton candy at a theme park, blissfully unaware of the shit-show life really holds. Just the sticky, sugary mess coating your fingers, licking it clean, and worrying about only one thing: which ride to go on next.

At some point, my elated spell began to fade, and I started to beat myself up whenever I felt anything other than ecstatically happy, indebted views to life's blessings.

If I failed to be grateful for all I had, fear crept in—warning me of a domino effect of negatives if I did not cling to this extremist, top-of-the-world, paradise-like appreciation, with the potential to return to old routines.

For this joyous state to be achieved, without a doubt, I had to give up the saucy-sauce, cold turkey. The on-the-wagon stints lasted anywhere from four days to three months. I already had an inkling of how withdrawal symptoms would feel—you never forget your first—I had my first two-ish week sober cleanse at twenty-nine years old after immense abuse since fifteen after Royal Hell.

Incipiently, my temptations didn't fade right away, mostly because I had only skimmed the crust of my own f*cked-up-ness.

I did not have the faintest idea of what I was in store until my 'Mo-Psychological Due Diligence Plan' was officially in the works.

As one might expect, I relapsed many times with the vicious cycle of self-hatred going with it.

This tranquilized state of mind gave me the means not to think about what had taken place in my life. Alcohol, combined with the severity of the traumas, subconsciously suppressed my distressing experiences.

Blackouts deepened a cycle of dissociative defense mechanisms, leaving me unable to access any memories or summon fearlessness to look at the beasts-of-my-life in the eye.

Given that I always put everyone else first while ignoring my own identity, I had no real conception of who I was at my core, or what I truly wanted to achieve in life.

From the get-go of self-healing, it seemed unattainable for someone like me to beat the statistics, as I told myself they existed for a reason. No one denies that the odds of overcoming childhood traumas are tough, but I had overlooked an importunate truth.

While the likelihood of my success wasn't in my favor—it was still achievable—if I could muster that hundred-eleven percent commitment and effort toward myself that I always gave to everyone else.

To truly get it right, I had to sort out my brain's dependence on alcohol to feel my abnormal-normal in order to function.

Even after two or three weeks of sobriety, my brain would hit a slump. Then, I would have a glass of wine to feed its craving and bam—suddenly, I was energized and ready to go. As if someone had knocked on my door, and—yep—she's home.

Almost like my organs were operating on a mix of thirty percent alcohol and thirty percent water. No matter how much water I drank, my brain chemistry remained off kilter until I gulfed down a trim level of alcohol.

Once I did, my mind and attention span kicked into a high-end performance mode, thanks to being 'clear-headed sober' for a season of time beforehand—if that makes any sense.

Then comes the taper-off situation with booze as I tried to navigate my way through a strange balancing act of cravings and lucidness.

The sugar urges were ferocious as my body reeled from the shock of losing the alcohol-induced sweetness it had come to depend on.

Bouncing back and forth like a tennis match—completely dry for a few weeks, then a light indulgence, only to swing back to a quick hello of desert-level dryness.

This cycle would increase to months, but either way, each day was an internal battle between good and evil as I kept seeking outwardly to fill my gaping voids.

When I sipped off-beat glasses of wine, guilt inflamed my carelessness—a sharp reminder of my failure to acquiesce the path toward a new version of myself.

Alcohol was a constant presence, whether I partook or not. I assured myself that one or two drinks would be fine since I felt healed enough not to spiral out of control.

Wrong, start the clock over again—*again*.

Either I was a hundo healthy or its polar opposite. There was no steady or middle ground, no balance.

This sweet talk to myself came as easily as turning a page in a book. Moderation was supposed to be the key to success, yet I remained stuck somewhere between stages three and four of healing.

The first doorway toward enjoining the bridge of my becoming—so that I may meet destiny with an open heart and a loving spirit—would be taking the indispensable step I had skipped: forgiving myself.

It was time for absolution, for the one who governs my gravity field: *me*.

And when that fateful day arrives and this bridge of life is tested, it will be built from *adamantine*. Never again will I allow myself to be serially manipulated, annihilated or burned by anyone.

At times, I cling to my victim mentality like a security blanket as wounds without justice, resolution, or safety keep me in a panic grip as if clamping down on an obsidian blade. Sharp enough to slice through bone, leaving brittle shards that re-shatter the broken pieces within.

My greasy-ass elbows were still on the table holding my chin up as I wallowed in the blame-game—a self-defeating, poor-me cerebral flow, while I hid all this internal pouting from the rest of the world.

These muscled-up arms needed to get to work and move the needle on the complex hatchling years—to take control of these trauma-survival statistics and swing things in my flavor-favor.

In an effort to get my ass in gear the

universe drop-kicked-me—it was a divine smack with a wake-up-wand to stop trippin' by and get my shit together.

Postponing this life through a dormant complacency, with an inebriated fog as I barely scraped by, was not it—my soul surpassed consent. It was time to wake-up each morning with fire in my veins, surging my momentum into the brilliance of my purpose. Better late than... *never*.

The jig was up. I had the grisly talk with myself once I informed the right side of my brain that it was not invited. My creative idea-machine would get its update on the next steps when the time was right.

Taking no prisoners, I went in for the kill to claim a win—to put an end to my weakling excuse of a life I kept repeating, until nothing remained in my soul but an unholy mess.

Eating my brutal biscuit, it dawned on me that I wasn't just living a masked double-life. It turned out I had three lives, or personalities, I should say.

All I could think of was *"This cannot be true. There is no way I am this higgledy-piggledy,"* prompting one of the sides of me to burst out laughing.

The inappropriate jokester was Side Two of me, chuckling at this here—Side Three's expense—given it took this long to identify that the first two of us were in cahoots.

Once I smacked and tapped these letters on the keyboard to see what words would stick, I decided to save a major trauma trait for the end as a surprise for you all—I am killin' it with more damaged qualities—you ain't got nothing on me.

Talk about finding someone who checks all the boxes. Well, psychological trauma boxes, that is.

There has been no lack of effort for me to recognize my faults, while I strictly hold my self accountable. However, this was a horse-sized vitamin I had to gavage—as if I were a duck being force-fed into foie gras—in order for me to digest this gorging party life and fluctuating selves.   304

It was now my curtain call to reveal the trinity sides of me and to bow out this final act. Taking this hard look at myself, I noticed the crusty-old-boogers in my nose, now that I wasn't focused on the snot dripping down someone else's.

The first thing was first. It was time to deal with all these multiple layers inside me, as if one identity was not enough.

Golly-jeepers.

The day of reckoning had arrived for me to dissect these numerous personalities and to stop the three of us from fighting over our own time in the spotlight.

At the very least, this was a staggering discovery.

Not only was it imperative to dispel the negative energies lurking within me, but it was also inescapable that I lay to rest the appalling traits within Sides One and Two of myself—to strive and follow what was—and is—steadfast in my heart: faith in life, and respect for human kind and animals.

Side One of me fictitiously acted based on everyone else's response: the resourceful, impostor syndrome extraordinaire, who was a versatile, perfectionist.

Now, this Side Two was a doozy. The one that periodically seeped through my pores, spewing red flares and hazard lights as warnings to those around me.

This unruly side was the incomplete, tragic child who lived a denial-riddled, lost and damaged life—a prisoner of lust, pride, wrath, sloth, greed and gluttony.

Each sin served as both a crutch and a chain, feeding chaos as it disintegrated every trace of growth—fueled by my Kung-Fu grip on instant gratification who *thrived* in self-destruction.

A walking billboard for the Devil himself.

Mercifully, envy has never been a part of my makeup—altruism and empathy have always been my redeeming qualities.

And then, there's my work-in-progress, Thrice Self as I like to call it.

The one building a firm foundation three times over, with a guarded and structured process. A self-inquirer ruled by integrity—highly motivated to improve each day, and dedicated to creating an ever-evolving, enhanced version of myself—now, and in the future.

On the unforgettable days that I diligently worked to transfer these words into a book, I was sucker-punched in my soul—in the most disgusting and inhumane way.

It was as though my life was quivering on the brink of... over. Every part of my being wishes I could say this was some wild, creative exaggeration.

But no, not in the slightest. These blows were fatal and left me utterly immobilized, with its death-grip tightening around the last scraps of sanity I had left, after these audaciously absurd trespasses into my world.

Frozen, in an extended period of shock, with no wherewithal to move, all I could do was stare up at the burnt bridge I had righteously lit, crying to myself:

"There is no way things can get any worse. I have to make them stop! I can't take it anymore..."

This overpass of mine was drenched with accelerants—hacked and possibly still being surveilled through my phone, laptop and other Bluetooth-enabled devices.

All for that click—click—boom—revenge. And, of course, to ensure I don't write about them—that whole NDA thing.

Quick breakaway to chime in on how— Pelicans Tellin' Porkies —was born.

Why Pelicans? Well, the head honcho of this crafty gang of digital terrorists, owns a 'communications' company that has the name affiliated in it.

Porkies? To me, it's a hilarious British term for lies, and it softens the blow when I write about them. Call it my little linguistic gift to myself.

These deathly shadow walkers worked

tirelessly to strip away every ounce of my dignity in a profound way. The verdict is in, and there is no surprise here—they are over achievers.

At one point I literally, not figuratively—shook violently. Overtaken by terror-stricken nerves—overwhelmed by shallow breaths—I was mentally barricaded within their horror show.

The crushing realization hit me: I was trapped with nowhere left to turn, having drained every last tax-funded resource that I knew of at the time.

No joke, sarcasm, or reading between the lines there. This whole fiasco proves to me that their swamp pockets run as deep as the bummock of Iceberg-A23a.

I shudder to think about what we're not privy to, even though we are now seeing a minor bit unfold in a digestible amount—trickled out to soften the blow for those who do not indulge in 'conspiracy theories.'

Despite the evidence I had, not one person

would listen to me and investigate to save me from the inevitable mental breakdown. It is extremely alarming and concerning how far these Pelicans went to try and silence me.

What's more terrifying is the amount of power they yield and the influence they possess which spans multiple jurisdictions and entities.

Thankfully, they all counted their gram bags and cocaine bricks before they started slangin.'

As I lay helplessly in my prematurely dug grave, shell-shockingly-desperate when I was close to giving up due to their multi-layered maneuvers to silence me for good.

This excessively immoral invasion of my life, and the ignored lawlessness behind this ruthless small-town espionage and censorship is incredibly annoying.

They are outpacing justice thus far, and I bet my life these Pelicans will continue to diabolically and perversely devastate anyone who does not have their interests aligned with these sleazeballs, not just me.

An attorney who once revised my late Oma's will, Trevor Zink in San Jose, CA, became a curious figure that was in my life more than I signed up for.

I must speculate the exact timing of my email to him since the Pelicans conveniently erased it from my account. But, I am pretty certain it was Sunday, November 27, 2022, around 9:00 PM PT.

I reached out to Trevor and asked if we could discuss my gruesome situation. I kept the email vague because who leads with:

"Hi, my life has turned into a Netflix thriller, and unbeknownst to me, you are probably a supporting character, yet to be confirmed?"

To my surprise, Trevor responded the next morning, the 28th, around 9:00 AM PST—offering me a choice of either 3:00 and 3:30 PM that same day.

Part of me hadn't expected such a prompt reply, so I never had a chance to read his email before the call. The other part was tangled up in my complicated relationship with technology and my insufferable avoidance of it.

To my astonishment and minor horror, Trevor called me at the time he suggested. I laid it all out: the nefarious, borderline of unbelievable things that had transpired.

They put Jeffrey Epstein's picture as app icons on my iPad. I immediately snapped photos of it with my phone, but within a minute, the Pelicans deleted. It was as if my phone had been mirrored and their version overrode mine.

Every app, every action, everything I did—they interfered with.

Pelicans blocked access to accounts. Updated my profiles with old, inactive phone numbers, and emails while flashing scary warnings onto my screen.

The Pelicans intercepted my calls to Chase

and the Monterey Police, dropping creepy lines like *"Check your brakes,"* or *"You need burial insurance."*

While I slept, I played relaxing nature sounds through Spotify's app—only to hear eerie noises and familiar voices mixed in. They spoke to me in my sleep and jolted me awake in sheer terror.

They sent burial emails and spoke through my laptop and phone—tossing in insults like *"psycho."*

How *hilarious...* I was the one being gang-stalked, tormented, and micromanaged into a dissociative collapse, but I am the psycho?

Okay—got—it.

Trevor's Response: *"Don't worry, this happens all the time. They won't physically hurt you. They are just trying to scare you, so you don't sue them. This usually lasts about a year, so that you will be exhausted, and you won't have a legal standing to go after them.*

I had a client go through the same situation, and the things these hackers can do are insane with the technology that is out there right now. It made them miserable, but they eventually got through it."

It makes me wonder—was there a possibility that Trevor's client wanted to sue someone? Him, perhaps? Not that it was my place nor intent. But what if, in retaliation, these Pelicans hacked and terrorized Trevor's client?

Hey, Trevor's client—sound familiar?

When we signed with Trevor for the will, he boasted how he visits Carmel often—and according to an online search, his work partner went to school in Pebble Beach.

At the crux of it all, how could Trevor possibly know beyond a shadow of a doubt, that these Pelicans wouldn't escalate their antics into something physically harmful, than what they had already inflicted?

Love me a hypothetical: What if Trevor has a personal or business relationship with one of the Pelican's?

By law, doesn't a lawyer have an obligation

to report when someone's life is being threatened? Especially if that person is so scared for their safety that they draft a contingency kill-switch to hand over, in case they're silenced for good?

How could Trevor say without a shadow of a doubt I would not be physically harmed *without-knowing* who was targeting me—that cyberstalking was just a scare tactic?

The State Bar of California—what's your take on this? Do you step in if a lawyer is a known participant in illegal activity? Any progress with the March 2025 complaints?

Let me tell you, about three weeks after my call with Trevor, someone tried to run me over with their car.

Right outside my house. On a quiet street. I was standing by my car, clear as day, and the driver was looking right at me. Giving a polite neighborly hat tip, I glanced over—until he gunned it—full throttle, veering his car directly toward where I stood as I jumped in my car.

One second later, I would not be here today—and I followed him for his plate.

This whole situation shakes me to the core. At times it makes me doubt my ability to stay positive and keep the faith that I'll overcome it and fully heal.

But then my stubborn streak kicks in with an unshakable determination to fight-the-fight, as I am reminded of one undeniable truth: I never want these Pelicans to have the chance to terrorize someone else or destroy another life.

Their last-ditch effort to intimidate me into ceasing my willingness to secure help from anyone—the exact day could be confirmed via body cam videos, but it was about the middle of August 2023.

When I walked through the living room and saw my reflection in the window as I sipped my coffee, I noticed a red light on my chest—I looked down and confirmed the tactical sight—my everything went blank, dark—only to freeze my heart in time.

There is no other way for me to describe it other than the visceral certainty that I was about to be murdered—instantly flooded by a dense emptiness, and an acceptance within the eviscerating shock that my life, as I knew it, was *over.*

As I said to myself, *"Oh God. This is it. They are really going to put me down. This can't be happening right now."*

As I prayed to God, I asked if the Pelicans could strike me directly on the heart, so I would go quickly and *painlessly*—as I ran and hid in the closet of my bedroom hysterically crying. With whatever scraps of brainpower I could call upon, I tried my best to hold my sanity together.

It's insane to think about all the pockets being lined through illegal dealings. They're greasing their wheels with their accomplices, who have sunk so deep in quicksand, that all they can do now is cling to their thin, plausible-deniability existence.

Because, let's face it—if even one of them

goes down, the whole web of players would unravel. The fallout would be catastrophic for them—f*ckin' brilliant sequel for me.

Little mind-boggles with this one: All that money. All that time. All that work poured into careers, licenses, and public stock markets—and yet they still have the cojones to gamble it all on Person-One hearsay—town gossip—for retaliation that was built on grossly wrong assumptions.

It's like they're playing high-stakes poker with someone else's chips, with no idea what's in their hand.

The funniest part is that I had zero intention of writing about them or their oh-so-precious NDA drama. But look at us now—a little switchback swerve from the conniving *lawipulators*—to an underdog story that will cut the Vipers' tail clean *off*.

And, as if things were not messy enough, they decided to throw even more people into the mix—chef's kiss.

based on the Omni of their corruption, my Mission is clear: i am All-Red, to throw Ranch and a Pebble at this Beach with my unapologetically *bizarre* 11th-Hour Coffee. one thing's for sure—i will not Alter my Call.

C L I N K - I T T Y . . . CLINK. CLINK.

Straight to the Pokey-Poke.

Heavens to Betsy, this is Bloody Hell—Satan must be absolutely beaming over his Dirty Bobby's and Wicked Sidekicks.

I cut everyone out of my life after this, even though I did not *Juan* to.

The concentration of my spirit had to be centered on celestially fashioned frameworks with no distractions—hibernation mode was in full effect.

While in my dormancy, it came to a point where I did not have one ounce of energy to function. It was a paralyzing, debilitating existence.

No bother of messes around the house since I had zero shits to give.

In bed for days on end—well, I say days, but it was months of doing even less than the bare minimum, given I was asleep more than awake. The chronic, bone-deep stress had me molting, with my face aging like a three-centennial witch who lost all of her powers.

Walking around looking like Gollum from Lord of the Rings. Thank goodness for hats, sunglasses, and hair extensions.

It took eight months before I was able to start reading this again to slowly work on refinements. Being on a laptop—or even a phone, for that matter—freaked me out.

I was nowhere near ready to face what came after publishing this in 2023. There was no emotional reasoning. I subconsciously erased any and all memories for my own survival since the anguish was simply too devastating for me to process.

Even now—over two years later—I am only slightly comfortable, but extremely hyper-vigilant, saving my writing in every place I can think of.

I tried my best to recall all the original funnies erased, but it only backfired on them—granting me a fiercer tenacity and will to make the phantom of the mind come true.

All their efforts to not let my work see the light of day inspired me with ingenious ideas, if I do say so myself.

Now to the point where I had enough of this deplorable life I was living, God was all I could think of.

With a sincerity I had never known, I prayed to God with all my might. It wasn't the frantic *"I'm about to die,"* kind of prayer, but a true and measured plea. I didn't ask for an escape, but for a path—one that would let me save myself with every ounce of mettle I had left.

In the face of these scandalously vile afflictions, I begged for His reinforcement to be triumphant over it all.

By the Grace of God, I was saved. A relationship with Him became the ultimate victory in disguise from this nightmare.

Had those Pelicans not desecrated me with their expertly trained psychological warfare, I might never have reached out to Him. Their cruelty drove me to seek His divine guidance to harness perseverance and carve out a path to rescue myself.

God saved me from withering away, from wasting the air I breathe, the talents I have been given, and the open-ended heart I carry to help others in need.

Before I even opened the Bible, I quit my substance vices—freely, willingly, and without hesitation. I was thirsty for full control over my flesh and to purify my life.

Shortly after making this glorified commitment, it was as though my choice was divinely confirmed.

Faith stands as a fortress, unshakably fueled by a ferocious will to fulfill my soul and to let self-love with respect reign everlastingly.

Methodically, I examined myself to trace the fractured lines that define me, to uncover whether I possess the internal power to love myself unconditionally. All so that I could find a way to accept the devious-dickens of our world without ever condoning them.

In doing so, this allowed me to take a scalpel to my own psyche and work toward forgiveness within myself—for my own sake, not theirs—and then, ultimately, let go of the afflictions that hindered me.

Success in my finite, starlit gravity field will be my revenge. Eye-for-eye vengeance is a cycle that never ends. I have ample energy for today but—*almost*—none for yesteryear. Besides, retribution isn't mine to claim.

It's God's turn now to take over my final act of redemption which is a now pending, **Federal Lawsuit 5:25-cv-09710-NC** [copy on my website], and see through the restoration of my dignity.

When He steps in, they will no longer be deceptively botching up my world and poisoning the 'water-in-my-well.'

Oh, what a glorious day it will be when

God's wrathful furies rain down upon Satan and his followers, as they perish beneath the weight of their own wickedness.

It was time to let go of what once had me like glass under snow—to call out Satan and his ways—and, even more so, to refuse to abide by his destructive design.

So, I handed in my resignation for the last time, vowing never to look back. It was at this moment my life's taxes were being put to beneficial use.

While working for the Beast, he assumed that the rot on my hands—the wear and tear from the endless tasks I completed at his command, came at no cost to me.

Once I said goodbye to Lucifer's ways, a white light pierced through my being and delivered me radiantly at peace. It was time to be filled with His grace, gladness, and lionheartedness.

As I move through this life in God's hands, I like to cast a mental scene that the stains on my soul are being scattered with every blink of my eyes.

The blasphemy that once clouded my mind? Discarded. Gone. As though it never belonged to me in the first place. I stood firm and uplifted—cleansed, renewed, and guided by His light.

For the next part of my spiritual process, I visualized the lifelong sins and demons that once devoured my being, were scorched away by the cleansing rays of the sun.

These impurities, once exposed to light, transmute into a swarm of what can look like three million bats fleeing their cave at sunset—in a wild, relentless rush.

Then, this filth shoots up a black tunnel streaked with gray shadows, disappearing without a trace as it scatters and races toward a quick, deceitful flash of white light—a false beacon that lures them in.

Only to find that it's the dirty Devil himself, masquerading as an angel, waiting to claim the Earth's tormentors.

In a divine symphony, mesmerizing and mystic, supernatural rocks—bluish-gray on the outside, pulsing with God's radiant white light at their core—avalanche in a 360-degree protective barrier—a sacred fortress around the newly saved.

Now cleansed, the darkness within has been cast out. But no soul will ever be seamless. There will always be cracks where shadows might creep back in, should one falter in their devotion.

God celebrates these victories, as His flock cheers of joy seethe through the Beast's blazing, lava-filled lair.

The Devil now grieves the loss of yet another soul—saved by the One. The Only. The Almighty King.

The green-eyed demons floated alongside Satan, shivering with fear—quakin', shakin', and bakin'. The Fallen One is now in God stricken horror and despair, desolated by the bitter taste of defeat as the spiritual war has fully commenced.

And just like that, it was time for me to head east to leave behind the Pelicans' heavily booby-trapped, corrupt-California resources and step into a new, untainted way of living.

When the time is right, righteous rain will cascade, baptizing the world in justice. On that battle-blessed day, I shall sit back, relax, and rejoice in the byproduct of divine vengeance and wrath.

At the drop of a tanning-oil-bottle, my life began to shift. The moment my plane landed, everything started to change, steering me in the right direction—for the first time in my life.

I find myself cheerfully disgusted now that I can see things for what they are. Even amid the rubble of my pulverized world, I remain eternally thankful to be alive.

Gratitude is my lifeline even as I struggle most days to rebuild my life from scratch. Daily battles will dwindle to battle, then to pure serenity in life one day.

Everything that I practiced before— harnessing positive vibes, showing kindness without the Karen-level shade, no matter how they treated me, while prioritizing healthy routines, suddenly clicked into place.

From there, I incorporated Epsom salt baths infused with spirit-lifting aromas. A sacred ritual for cleansing and shedding the diabolical energies that weigh me down, as if I were a holistic crystal fresh from a séance—purged of darkness, reborn in light.

I now smell like a walking-day-spa.

Hit with a clarity wave and my third eye opening, I cooked up probing journal prompts to plunge into the depths of my psyche—scrutinizing every angle of my life to unwrap the truths I had long avoided.

For the most tragic, unhealed pieces of my life, I remain on the daunting road, searching for whatever gold lies buried in the rubble. For God has been the only silver lining to surface within the Pelican's perfidies, yet to be healed.

The driver's seat of my life will be reclaimed when I naturally live each day as I elevate peacefully.

ELEVATE:

Empowered. Liberated.
Enlightened. Vibrantly. Authentically.
Tenaciously. Emboldened.

PEACEFULLY:

Purposeful. Empathy. Ambitious. Centered.
Encouraged. Fulfilled. Unburdened.
Limitless. Love. Yourself.

Next, I had to address the wear and tear of my consumption that had my body crying out for: magnesium, folic acid, iron, zinc glycinate, and complex B vitamins.

Based on my vast testing of chemicals for these altered states of consciousness, I researched natural ways to replenish serotonin and dopamine.

Many of the cognitive blends overlapped with vitamins I had already purchased. Buying each separately is pricier, but it's more precise and lets me fine-tune the specific needs of my health regimen.

Everyone's chemistry sings different tunes, so please consult a doctor first. I am only sharing what helped me personally, *not* offering medical advice.

Hands down—L-Methylfolate, B9 and B12 with active 15 mg—is an absolute miracle for my mood. I began slowly with only three **single drops** under my tongue once a week, then twice a week—**not** the whole dropper.

Shilajit wiped out my brain fog the first time I took it. It's potent stuff, so I started at 0.25g once every three weeks for several months before bumping it up to once a week still at the same dose.

Each of the following supplements have also been instrumental in fueling my holistic well-being, restoring and revitalizing my all:

Tryptophan, 5-HTP, Rhodiola Rosea, Huperzine A, L-Theanine, L-Tyrosine, SAMe, Taurine, GABA, Berberine, Ginkgo Biloba, Lion's Mane, Ashwagandha, Milk Thistle, Oregano Oil, Dandelion, Olive Leaf Complex, Black Walnut.

I place a heavy emphasis on daily exercise. Carving out time for consistent workouts that not only energize me but also overflow my cheerful glass to the brim, spilling positivity into every nook and cranny of life.

Physical conditioning motivates so that I steer clear of self-sabotage. It equips me to wrangle and tackle the daily horsing around, while I ride the wild bucks thrown my way.

No squandering calories on junk food—well, except for the occasional treat. Poor eating habits turn me into a mashed couch potato, with my gravy brain dribbling and seeping through the cracks of life.

One of my least favorite lessons was not just accepting that it's healthy and natural to cry, but to also embrace it. Allowing myself to experience and process those touchy-feely emotions when they came fighting to the surface, without shutting them down at the onset.

To sob at all, I first had to grab my traumas by the throat and stare them down head-on without flinching.

Time to squeeze out the psychological defense mechanisms that had always driven me to deny, repress, rationalize, and displace.

There were no breaths left, no capacity within me to keep avoiding the inner work.

For far too long I had stifled the natural reaction to weep, given that I was trained to *man-up-and-take-it*. Never to allow myself to charter the uncharted ways of feeling-the-feels, in feelings.

Pretending that "*I am strong, I can handle it,*" without ever acknowledging the truth, I created an atmosphere of emotional numbness within the shadows of my world.

While writing, I stifled the urge to cry. There have been plenty of drunken tears and reactionary outbursts in the past, but they were drowned beneath reality erasers and blurred by a chemical haze. There was never any depth, just hollow emotions left uncontested.

At last, I ultimately said *"Screw it. I have nothing else to lose."*

I removed my lacrimal glands belt—and let-it-all-hang-out. I was a blubbering fool, panting while bawling my eyes the heck out, as my emotional floodgates gave way.

Releasing all that wet salt was liberating. The intricacies of my triple threat personality I exhumed were now illuminated. These Fort Knox level emotional walls that once blocked any instinct to cry were remarkably... eradicated.

Shedding those tears with intention was the most disentangled step in my journey to close my childhood wounds at a faster rate—without a doubt.

No more locking and stuffing life inside Pandora's Box-of-Pain, waiting for another travesty to explode. No more smoldering fire of a thought process poisoning my bloodstream with emotional cyanide.

Although I am free from my wee-lassie wounds, I still wrestle with the Pelican's conscience-shocking violations.

It still feels as though my everything was

beaten by metal baseball bats: full-body, inside-out, life-ending pain that lacerated my nerves, soul, heart and mentality, debilitatingly deep.

And I sure as hell did not see that aftermath coming.

Never was I one to have insomnia before, but I now find that poor sleeping is a normal routine. Being a morning person has always been a strong suit, even when hungover—but now, I have taken it to an ironic level.

These days I start my mornings around the same time I used to end my nights—one to five—back when I was guzzling alcohol and whatever else that came my way.

Scripture is my priority of the day even over caffeine. Once I am in tune with the Holy Trinity, then bring on the exercise of extended endurance runs during sunrise.

Game changing way of life now. My mind is calmer, and I can handle almost anything with a newfound sense of ease by nurturing my physical and psychological well-being.

how to deal with and balance out my slight touch of a narcissistic attitude—since "I am always right"—but with the mantra: "I can take on anything. I am fine. Don't worry about me. How can I help *you*?"

am I short-tempered if hungry? Do I need to stress over things I *have no control over*? Only *me* to look out for—*you*, side three.

i have a snappy, sappy, and scrappy attitude from being tired, and will *lose* it from pent-up energy because I did not workout.

doing self-realization tests, I *watch me* become more flustered when I do not exercise. It causes me to *incinerate* into a touchy-touchy temperament if I am not getting my heart rate up. *And*, it is all thanks to the ton of natural energy I possess.

pebble sized emotions may linger, but I will *reveal* my vigor effectively, or *your*s truly will erupt into a *full-blown* explosion. my emotions will spiral *out-of-control*, and my *actions* will be *led by ego*.

beach jogs are a must, with body weights on light walks.

335

AND... SCENE.

The writing you aren't reading—that's the lemon to my honey water.

This war-of-words pocketbook in your phalanges—it's my compass, guiding me through the open seas of the world-play of words:

Cleverly captivate curious cerebrals with charm and compassion, by courageously crafting a comedic cast into the complexities of life.

Lifelong teaching lesson seeds that others planted and are now sprouting—they're the sweet-scrumptious apples growing on my tree.

Revisiting my life through the lenses of others has become my way of uncovering hidden blessings—energizing insights that inspire me to pursue growth each day that I wake up.

As I sharpen my discernment, every fresh perspective fuels my powerhouse-'n'-holy edition. Like brain boosting fatty-fish sparking love in my heart, surging artistic mojo to my inner muse, and hatching visionary flow straight through my hands.

When the time is right, I will lighten the load for others in a restorative way—only, if it does not harm me in the process.

Journaling has been nothing short of alchemy. I highly recommend giving it a go if you're yearning for an outlet to meet more of the divine you.

One thing that's never changed about me?

I cannot stand being told that I am incapable of doing something, especially when I have set my sights on it. For as far back as I can remember, I always resisted anyone's attempt to dominate me—even when they succeeded.

The difference now is I no longer let their disbelief fuel my need to prove them wrong. There is no need for extra gusto from negativity. I operate at my maximum level of effectiveness, for me.

Removing my emotions from others' doubts or cynical reactions to avoid hostility has been a peaceful way for me to get my shit done every day. Rarely does my skin break open, as the salt burns my flesh.

Indulging in other people's complaints of misery with no constructive end game?

The f*ck I will—will not. No seconds will be given to letting their bullshit tamper with my cognitive flow. Whenever adverse ideas or reactions leave me flurried or conflictingly excited—I take a step back, stop what I am doing, and settle-in-stillness before I even think about responding.

Time to breathe before taking a bite— striving to be rational and processing before reacting. Whether it's their last word, or a passive-aggressive text or email slide in, I refuse to be pulled into their chaos.

This approach allows me to stay calm and carry on, reducing the chance of impulsively misspeaking, as I activate my Devil's advocate mindset.

Although, I am far from perfect—I am imperfectly perfect—there will always be a slip-up of some sort. But, I refuse to restrict myself within the narrow confines of *"I-am-right"* tunnel vision. This trap blindsided me into a brick wall, given that I was driven by my ego, lack of boundaries and self-love.

The victory in camouflage will unearth itself once I have identified the deeper insight that is key to comprehending the lesson.

Every day I pray the eye of the storm has finally passed—but only God is privy to their antics, as I sift through the wreckage of the crash-and-burn landing.

It took two years to reach a place where I can confidently say I survived—but I am far from healed—and I did it without relying on anxiety meds or antidepressants. There were, however, a few sporadic bouts with alcohol along the way.

Going without medication or speaking to a professional was not by choice—and I don't recommend my route to anyone.

For a moment, I joined Cerebral's services for one of my urgent requests, hoping to find the support I so desperately needed. The counselor I spoke with assured me they had the resources to help navigate the Pelican's calculated devastations. I should add that he made me feel confident that I found my outlet for emotional support.

On the other hand, the psychologist gave her oath the middle finger—dismissed me entirely and said I was *paranoid* and *"We can't help you here"*—shaming me that it was all a figment of my imagination.

Pelican connection—or reach?

It took about a week to get assigned to a psychologist, all while every move was being monitored online. And let's get one thing straight—it's not a delusion when I have proof. Most critically, they never would have tried to silence me if I were making things up.

The ultimate core takeaway is—I jumped off that hamster wheel, and my psychological armor is strapped and ready to go.

No more drowning in alcohol to forget what my life once was or is. I try to wake up each morning excited to start the day and bring my ideas to life.

Above all, I am embracing my present and future by honoring myself. Alcohol holds no dominating hold over me. I can go months without it, and its absence will never again dictate my mood or mental state.

Celebratory glass of fermented grapes? Yes. I am graciously gratified that I never want more than two—booze is not a priority, hobby, or source of joy, whatsoever.

What purely ignites me is my faith in God, exercise, nourishing food to make me feel incredible—and of course—tapping these digital keys and scribbling by hand.

That's where my passion lives, and I have deemed it... Bold Chaos Theory. Which is based on my musings on life and the world: past, present, and future.

Healing from childhood trauma has restored me. I deeply look forward to each day now that I became the version of myself that I once admired in others—one I never imagined to be feasible for me.

Watching the sunrise is one of my favorite parts of the morning. When the sun starts to peak, I celebrate my 'giggle time,' now that I wear my dignity proudly and envision the fruits of praised works ahead.

Through it all, I tried my best to tread lightly while expressing my firm conviction that I was saved by the Grace-of-God, knowing full well that this is not the path for everyone.

Before this rebirth, I was spiritual but not a follower of Him—so, I get it. My sincere hope is not to come off like I am trying to shove anything down. This is simply the formula that solved the complex equation of my life.

The fact that I will soon be meeting with an atheist, I put deep thought into this part. If they read what I have *whimsically* slapped together, it will serve as a twofer: offering an explanation of my paradigm while providing a glimpse into my Christ-Centered, Light Walker Path.

Here's the thing—I keep an open mind to it all, even if others' views clash with my own. That willingness tempers the creeping arrogance of know-it-all tendencies.

I will never turn away from counsel, even when I can take a sound course of action on my own. Why not be open to another opinion, and give my honest attention to whoever is speaking?

There are days when I am not in the mood to talk to people, but I remind myself *"I like it when others honestly listen to me."* The perfect nudge to stay respectful, and more often than not, when I engage, it snaps me out of the downer my mindscape was in.

Gaining knowledge for me isn't about having blind, conformist trust or consuming information just because it's spewed at me. It's about challenging, filtering, and refining.

For example, I can lend an ear to the

news—not to regurgitate it as my own view, but to sift through differing interpretations, weed out the propaganda, and extract what sharpens my mind and opens my eyes.

It will never make sense for me to shun a book based on my not agreeing with the author's personal views. Even though their topic is right down my alley, and they are compelling writers who have me fully intrigued by their work.

There is no way I can make a blanket statement claiming that the California government and the executives running influential companies are corrupt—especially if I did not reside or work there my whole life, and only visited once, on a rushed Mission to try an exceedingly overrated restaurant that serves rat-poo infested bread to their customers while warning the staff not to eat it.

The firm stances I take on my quest for a virgin-brained adventure keep me grounded in my commitment to an unlatched, mental attic—I remain open to all viewpoints, no matter their origin, my preconceived notions, or societal pressures.

This approach does not seem to have a downside to me. Either way, I will find something new to contemplate at the end of the conversation.

Now, in terms of the Bible, can I disagree with some portions? Absolutely. I respect everyone's relationship choices.

Respect *only,* if you're **NOT**: a repugnant, revolting, grotesque, disturbingly-disgusting, child-molesting perving-predator, vile minor attracted grooming-pedophile, or a woman raping and beating—piece of f*ckin' shit scumbag.

Yes, I ask God every day for forgiveness for my potty mouth and then some.

Immersing myself in the word of God as I commit wholeheartedly to Him—due to my rightfully so, fear of God—is who I praise for my successes. He made me not want to give up on myself, my life.

An insincere, 'complimentary' shout-out to the Pelicans—your relentless torment that drove me over the edge, terrifying me to my core, and left me with nowhere to turn: You inspired me to pray, as I begged God to save me from the wreckage you caused.

So, here is my back-handed-F*ck... I mean, thank you for breaking me. You introduced me to thee almighty Himself, who is leading me to build an idolized life.

Sorry God, not there yet.

Moments after my first prayer, it felt as though God gently lifted my soul, wrapping me in His comfort. His undeniable presence assured me that He heard my cry—to lean on Him—with a little faith and a lot of effort, all will be brilliantly on point.

Now, for the incandescence of my existence: Living Over Easy in the Yolk of Life—Self-Mastery with God's Guidance.

To me, this means embodying self-love, humility, hope, self-discipline, unity, respect—self-and-others—and true forgiveness.

By striving for ethical honesty, establishing boundaries, practicing even-handedness, embracing maturity, and vanquishing life's challenges.

With a firm belief in these principles: fostering faith to affirm stability; avoiding shaming and exacerbating others or myself; embracing oneself through righteousness; upholding dignity with balanced asceticism; maintaining level-headedness with self-evaluation at the forefront.

These values guide me toward a balanced and meaningful life.

Flipping my switch to a healthy ambiance, I powered down the indulging sinner. This seismic shift suits my extremist personality—like bacon suits a dog's soul.

No matter how hard I try, I will never be perfect—and that's more than acceptable. It's within these imperfect pieces that I extract wisdom, compelling my inner luminary to fuel my vibez.

The various life lessons have instilled in

me to live with this attitude: I always win while learning. No such thing as losing or failing. Only opportunities to decondition negative thought patterns and habits while evolving from setbacks, hardships, and those so-called mistakes.

I choose to be ignited by these challenges rather than dwell on them, recognizing the invaluable knowledge they carry. But no participation trophies—time to get back to f*ckin' work.

Accepting flaws is the path to unlock life's blessings. Without it, life will feel like a roller coaster I accidentally jumped on as I whip and spin out of control.

I trust myself with each passing day now that I am armed with this hard-earned, extensively-expensive-expertise.

Life's toolbox will be enthusiastically ripped open to see what nuts to bolt, now that self-improvement and mini successes are mine to claim... One sneeze at a time.

No more acting like a petulant parasite,

draining the minds and energy of everyone involved. No more vengeful thoughts. No more hiding under blankets in the fetal position, head tucked low, eyes burning from the somatic pain and endless tears wishing my world would end.

Time to channel all my energy, mental acuity, and true grit toward the ultimate goal: an opportunity to reanalyze my original plan, refine it, and execute an outcome even greater than I imagined in the first place.

There is no space in this dome for self-imposed loathing, restrictions, and remorse. All will be corrected in its own time.

The Pelicans who dismantled my life, will no longer control my next move. The traumas I have endured and prevailed over—*will never*—define me.

What truly matters to me is cultivating and developing an unshakable, steadfast love, for the magical Father, His Son, who are the Sun. To live a radiant life that I deserve—a life we ALL deserve. With no explanation as to why...

BFD³

Believe. Feel. Demonstrate.

I *believe* in my value.

I *feel* my true worth.

I will *demonstrate* respect for myself at all times, including those around me.

Blessings. Faith. Discipline.

Life is full of *blessings,* even when the rays of sun behind the clouds are not visible at that precise moment. It will be undoubtedly clear when it is my time to understand what I could not see before.

Unshakable patience is key to it all. Life's advantages are only known to me when I take things in stride.

I will unfailingly keep the *faith* that all will work out—no matter the obstacles—now that I have the tools to be victorious.

I vow to stay *disciplined* for my mental and physical health, because I love and respect myself, and I deserve to live this life in serenity.

Because I Am—You're...

A Big Fuckin' Deal.

True Forgiveness Through Acceptance

After deep soul-searching under God's watchful eyes—spit-firing an array of dire prayers—I was unable to find it within myself to truly forgive those who upended my life.

I no longer believe I am meant to forgive in the sense of erasure or absolution, but rather to accept, without removing consequence.

For me, I cannot say I forgive someone while I look forward to, and work toward, justice—not to be confused with revenge, but with accountability, boundaries, and the refusal to carry what was never mine to bear.

True forgiveness, to me, in the traditional and biblical sense, requires both inward and outward release, with no lingering negative emotions that disrupt my inner peace—as if those slick bastards defiled my life yesterday, and I were still a raging, distressed ball.

The instant my first reaction becomes these three U-Motions[3]:

Unruffled, Undisturbed, and Unflappable, when speaking about my traumas or encountering the people who caused them, that will be my sign that I have succeeded.

So, why have I decided to hand out this clemency like a free appetizer on a wharf?

After three one-sided conversations with myself, I convinced us that I was not letting them win the war—after they already won the battles. I had no option left but to wave the white towel, surrender the fight, and redirect my focus inward.

Choosing to live in hatred toward Dad and others only ended up punishing me— not any of them. I sabotaged what micro amount of emotional health and general well-being I tried to foster my whole life.

No matter how violating or vilifying their actions were, I allowed them to destroy me, by weaponizing my own mind against myself.

I handed them the war of my life on a platinum platter, while I threw my sanity into a wood-chipper. All I truly accomplished was facilitating my own self-destruction, with far less effort on their part than what I put myself through.

There will be no guilt—no doubt—when I apply and expand this acceptance-based mindset. I will not feel shame for choosing to stand justly. Absolution is not mandatory for me to dispense, and that realization is mind-bending in the most liberating way imaginable.

Some will argue that the Good Book is firm on forgiving your enemies.

But to me, forgiveness implies the absence of penalties, the availability of my self to be taken advantage of again, along with the expectation of pretending that the damage was never catastrophic—while surrendering my dignity in the process.

True forgiveness, through acceptance, means there will be no revenge now or in the future. If they cross my path one day, I will be cordial. I will not go out of my way to hurt them—but I will not go out of my way to help them, either.

At the end of the day, we all sin, and when my time comes, I will ask for forgiveness for not forgiving my enemies, if it turns out that I am unable to do so.

I have unburdened the burdens of the past—pre-unburdened the burdens of the future—and outmaneuvered the maybe burdens before they even knew they were burdens.

No reapplying burden status just to unburden the burdens that have been over-burdened. Let us not forget the under-burdens that were balanced on the burden scale.

I walk so burdenless now that these burdens are relinquished—I blessed-em, flipped-em and sent them packing.

All it took was to stop feeding my ego, and quit treating my life like a casual game where the umpire and competing coach conspired to pull the victory out from under me.

No longer do I—*fully*—torture myself for not forgiving Dad before he was on his way to leaving this world. But admittedly, the thought still circles my mind, especially when I reflect on the meaning of life.

Although I made peace with Dad on his deathbed at the hospital—twelve hours before his soul let go of his body—I have only released *most* of my resentment toward myself.

The inability to have this conversation with him while he was alive remains a quasi-regret. I wish I had possessed this capacity for acceptance and true forgiveness back then, due to my rooted desire to help others heal based on my Bold Chaos Theory.

To have supported Pops on a path to a calm, peaceful, and joyful life would have been priceless. Deep under all that pain he felt inside, a good man was waiting to be freed and in control.

On the other hand, had I forgiven him in a typical conversation without the mindset of 'Self-Mastery with God's Guidance,' I doubt I would have reached this level of true forgiveness.

It's abundantly clear now that my journey was not about coming to terms with my reality and reconciling—it was about transforming myself. And that revamp would not have been plausible without the deeper understanding I have today.

At the heart of it, I refuse to be a bitter, crestfallen-critic, stewing in resentment—no matter the shady dealings done to me or others. Hate is a siphon of energy, a mental hoarder, leaving no room for the bliss-of-life.

Clinging to vitriol and animosity is like gripping an anchor—it drags me down, and drowns me in the depths of the past.

Here's how I see it: I have done some truly f*cked up things in my life. For those I have wronged, I can only hope they have forgiven me or accepted what has taken place—even if I will never know whether they, in fact, gifted any type of mercy.

How can I wish for that grace for myself, and not extend the same courtesy to others?

This isn't a tit-for-tat match-up of the

severity, either. True forgiveness doesn't work that way—no measuring wrong doings. Either you have it in you to truly forgive, or you don't—there are no halfsies.

Once I forgive, it is final. I will never throw it back in someone's face later—unless we have that relationship that thrives on sarcasm and embraces this type of playful exchange.

Forgiveness, for me, is a clean slate, not a lingering scorecard. Why not a fun example?

I will never stoop to dredge up a forgiven incident to stroke my ego, mentioning a past boo-boo, but my pride is really saying:

"Remember this? You messed up worse than me... I want you to relive the pain-you-caused, so I can keep the ball in my court—asshole."

That's not forgiveness, it is manipulation, and I am done playing those games.

On to my next—most important—point.

Nothing but love and respect for myself.

The only obligation I owe is to me—liable for my life, my choices, no one else. I flat-out refuse to wear others' yolks on my face for their actions.

There will be no second guessing what anyone says or does—they won't dictate the ingredients on life's menu or spice up the mood of my eternal cookout.

Hatred and revenge? No, thank you. I have no interest in being brined and vacuum sealed in spiteful resentment. Acting all salty, thirsting for revenge. Life's far too short for that kind of self-inflicted marinade.

Instead, I will rest easy-peasy, drifting into dreams of fresh words and alluring tales, wrapped in the peace that comes from embracing true forgiveness and self-care.

That said, when complications percolate and call for me to step in, I will rise to the occasion like shaving cream foam—ready and steady. With my new straight razor, I cleanly execute the task, leaving everything silky smooth.

All without letting my ego say a peep... although sometimes:

Side Two's Ego: *"Peep..."*

Thrice Self: "Nope, bye Felicia!"

Side Two: *"You just did a double André. Oh, I mean a double entendre. Well, now, I did a quadruple entendre. I am rubbing off on you Side Three!"*

No More Go Fish Moves... Chess, Baby!

Never again will I let anything weigh on my spirit, debating who is right or wrong. The only concern should be committing oneself to doing the right thing in life.

What did not happen often enough was acceptance of responsibility. Too often, my devilish ego took the reins, leading me down painful, superfluous roads. Been there. Done that. And I do not want to experience that turmoiled thought-stream *again*.

I want to be the kind of person others are proud to stand beside when life throws its next tangled wrinkle or unexpected snag. Not someone who comes out clean by bulldozing everyone else in the process.

Surviving the bottom-dwelling worst gave me an optimistic yet sensitive level of gratitude. One that provides a comforting protection I wear proudly.

In a wry twist, during tough times, I used to get highly annoyed when someone said, *"Everything happens for a reason."*

And yet, I now live by this adage until the stars fall—tracing the invisible thread for the divine message.

These incognito victories have been key to unlocking transformative insights—reminding me that even in life's nadir, there's always an actionable step waiting to sharply outline a new blueprint for living.

This mental defection I lugged around since I was a wee-lassie, somehow gifted me an amaze-balls lens to vivaciously appreciate the force of nature, the daily grind, and everything in-between.

The tiniest moments spark the utmost joy in my heart. My essence is tickled pink as easily as walking down the road, and a

car waves me through to cross the street—
sir, ma'am, you just made my day.

Opening a door for someone or letting them skip ahead in line because they have fewer items than me—*warm fuzzies.*

Chatting it up with the cashier while bagging my own groceries to make myself useful as we crack jokes to brighten our day—*tip-top, mic-drop.*

Experiencing all the considerate humans out there, adds that extra bounce to my pounce, knowing that we are not extinct. And, in fact—we are thriving.

I spit positive vibes and kindness to all, but I will never be impeccable, even with my exhausted efforts. High-highs will turn into low-lows. Every moment counts, so why not make it?

We will never know how One's hourglass was built. Nor when One's sand will run out. This is thee quintessential testament as to why my credence in the Holy Trinity's divine guidance is unwavering.

Now that I am immovably bound by His empowerment, I am free to truly seek in this world—so that I may—truly find.

Tranquil and steel-spined, I am comitted to embrace a life built on patience, nurtured by love, guided by faith, and shaped by true forgiveness at every step and...

Unmarked Road, Dead End, Cul-de-Sac, Wrong Way, Missed Exit, Fork-in-the-Road, Crash Barrier, Dead Man's Curve, Rock Slide, Lane Closure, Construction Zone, U-Turn, Dirt Road, Scenic Route, Tunnel, Overpass, Toll Booth, Checkpoint, Road Block, Bridge, Service Road, Pothole, Underpass, Fast Lane, Detour, Off Ramp, Divider, Median, Yield, Speed Bump, Oncoming Traffic, On Ramp, Guardrail, Stop-and-Go Traffic, Blind Curve, Carpool Lane, One Way, Railroad Crossing, Roundabout, Expressway, Merge, Crosswalk, Passing Lane, Gridlock, Hairpin Curve, Speed Trap, Hard Shoulder, Right of Way, Slow Lane, No Entry, Restricted Zone, School Zone, Freeway, Highway, Switchback and Z e b r a C r o s s i n g.

Rebirth Rhapsody

Time to peacefully exonerate yourself,
and those who defiled you...
by relinquishing the past,
from your hippocampus,
as you unchain the memory from misery.

The clock has spoken
for you to transcend from yesteryear,
by transforming life-lessons into wisdom.

Purify the pain by overcoming it,
once and for all.

The door stands open
for you to fuel your rebirth,
by cleansing what was
weaponized against you.

Thrive unapologetically,
by implementing your self-reflected truths,
and improvements,
in all aspects of your life.

The hour has come for you to prosper,
so that you may live a full-filled,
meaningful life.

To: young mo

Please, reach out to someone, you can't afford to waste any more time. Yes, you have unresolved trauma—issues that urgently demand your care and attention.

Your threshold has maximized beyond anything sustainable. It's time to begin your healing, so that you may uncover the truth of who you are and unleash your dazzling potential.

Mastering self-respect will be key in the life that you are manifesting. But first, you must nurture your inner rebel, starting with unflinching honesty about the pain-you-feel-inside.

Seeking life-saving guidance is **not** a shortcoming—it's a valiant, faith-driven step toward freedom. There are ample resources available for you. It's time to become fluent in the sublime of your mindset by reclaiming your power, once and for all.

You are the only one in your way. Daily personal growth is mandatory to break free of this dark cocoon.

Healing from abuse and life's bruises is yours for the taking—and I know you want it. Your idolized life journey begins with a single, powerful choice—a determination only you can make—no one else.

The life you want to wake up to every day is entirely in your hands. It depends on how badly you want it—because willingness or daydreaming is not enough.

You need to be starving for it. So hungry that you won't rest until you have feasted on the glaring meal of success.

You are not alone. Millions stumble down destructive paths, teetering on the brink of their last breath—only to hit rock bottom, wake up, and find the resolve to say:

"Not today, not ever. I will succeed because I am capable, and I can accomplish anything I set my sights on.

And... if I fall short, I'll return to the drawing board, craft a new plan, and use these lessons to fuel my comeback."

Pocket the following truths like armor because as you know... life will hit hard:

Commit to Yourself—Own the Process.

Dig-Deep—Push Your Limits—Reflect.

Learn from Your Mistakes.

Learn from Others F*ck Ups.

Decipher the Silver-Linings of Life.

Implement Self-Improvements.

Soar Beyond Your Boundaries.

Never Give Up.

Love Yourself.

You can do it, but it will demand every vertebra of your backbone to forgive yourself and work towards healing. That way, you can set your spirit free and ascend through this world without limits.

Work towards claiming the castle of talents bestowed upon you by the heavens, as you leave a trace mark within the vast breadth of your purpose.

Extending grace to those who have trespassed on your soul is not forgiveness nor absolution. It is simply acceptance so that you can release the weight of betrayal, allowing you to walk this earth unbound— no longer tethered to the annihilation and desolation born of their unconscionable actions.

This will be the path to achieving the highest goal of life: Serenity.

Please... Stop. Torturing. Yourself.

All that bullshit you crawled and withered through—everything you barely survived?

Those dark passages were not for nothing. They were your hands-on, real-world crash courses that will forge grit-built expertise once you apply yourself and harness that wisdom—acumen that will one day elevate you into being unstoppable.

Never disbelieve that you are valued, loved, and worth the effort. But remember, there are no shortcuts, no easy ways out.

Your dream life requires you to buckle the f*ck up—trust yourself—and get your ass to f*ckin' work!

I promise that you will not regret it. But hear this—it will not be simple or effortless, and it damn sure won't be handed to you.

It will be an exacting, inward pilgrimage through hell. Countless futile moments will grind you down until you're begging for mercy. This will be the most difficult endeavor your soul has ever urged you to undertake, and it will become the defining moment in which you finally earn the life you've longed to live.

On the other side of those soul-shaping growth-pains, lies a pot-of-gold kind of life filled with butterflies, rainbows, and a lux notebook paired with a platinum pen, now that you're ready to ink up your remarkable new world.

Impromptu for you

On the off chance anyone might find value in one of my trusty nuts that I have bolted down for self-discovery and healing deep trauma wounds, I decided to roll the dice and share them.

Here are a few—well, maybe a little more than a few—of my journal prompts that have aided-and-abetted my healing journey.

These considerations have taken shape over time as I continue to build upon them.

As I wrote in my responses, it became vital to pause and observe my psyche. I then read them aloud multiple times. It took a few rounds starting from the top before I could finish, as my own words often brought tears or gasps of breath.

When I was able to read them without breaking down, I looked at myself in the mirror and read them out loud, working hard to respect myself and to take it seriously.

I found that keeping eye contact was paramount for drawing my emotions out.

So, I scotch-taped my page to the mirror—finally, a proper use for tape.

It took a few tries to get the hang of it without completely losing it from laughing at myself. It was a turbulent sea of emotions between the tears, giggles, and that inner voice scolding and swearing that I was out of my mind for even trying this.

If you feel too numb or detached, give this a go:

What if the person you love most in the world trusted you with these emotions and experiences? What advice would you offer? How would you ensure they felt safe, valued, and cared for?

Now, can you use your own advice for yourself?

No More Tissues...
Let's Solve
Those Issues!

What are your triggers? Is there something no matter how small, it instantly sets you off?

For example: smacking gum, noisy eating, or slurping coffee. Does it bother you when everyone does it or a specific person?

If it's only one person, pause and reflect: Why does their behavior trigger such a strong reaction? What hidden emotions or past experiences might be fueling this?

What life situations are you avoiding or refusing to confront, and how might they have played a role in triggering this reaction?

What are the pros and cons of being hard on yourself?

What emotions make you uncomfortable or awkward? Can you pinpoint why you might be running away from this feeling?

In trying times when you rush, criticize or berate yourself, does it ever lead to a better outcome? How can you begin to show yourself more respect and compassion?

What do you offer to friends, family, and coworkers that you withhold from yourself? What would it look like if you extended that same kindness inward?

If you never belittle or patronize a child or anyone else, why do you do it to yourself?

What would change if you treated yourself with the same patience and understanding you give others?

What boundaries do you respect in others that you wish you could set for yourself?

What lines can you draw to ensure you feel respected, loved, and protected?

How might those boundaries bring you a more peaceful, patient mind?

How do your responses to your own needs change depending on who's involved?

What attachments make you feel safe? How do they shape your sense of security? What happens when you don't get what you want right away? How do you react?

Which forms of instant gratification do you crave, and are they truly healthy for you? Are these habits ones you feel proud of or do they hold you back, leaving you with that quiet sting of embarrassment afterward?

What are your strongest traits—the ones that have you walking on air, embodying the version of yourself you aspire to be? And what are the areas that still need your attention and care?

What parts of your personality do you like? Which ones challenge or frustrate you?

What are your weakest traits or what do you dislike about yourself?

What small yet consistent changes can you make each day that will create extraordinary results over time? Small actions each day will lead to a meaningful transformation.

How do you characterize and identify yourself? What words come to mind when you think about who you are?

What are some moments where you have trusted yourself fully?

What tools can you use to stay mindful and correct negative patterns or impulses?

What excites you the most about your future? What dreams put an extra bounce in your pounce?

What morals do you value most?

What three changes can you implement to truly live by your ethics? In other words, how can you practice what you preach?

What sacrifices do you make, who do you hurt, and what problems do you create to sustain your addictions?

This could include shopping, people pleasing, sex, unhealthy or co-dependent relationships, alcohol, drugs, food, nicotine, vaping. What would change in your life if you addressed these addictions?

How can you build self-care into your daily life to foster lasting change?

As you dissect your hardships, troubles, and traumas, can you find the silver lining in each?

How have those experiences taught you to persevere?

What will motivate you to push through life challenges?

How have these experiences humbled you and why?

What inner strength have you gained from finding these blessings in disguise?

How can you use these lessons to become more confident and better prepared for future bumps in the road?

Healthy Tree : Scrumptious Fruit

Intuitive self-care is all about listening, really tuning in to what your body is trying to tell you.

Which foods make me feel nourished, energized, or emotionally comforted? How do they affect your body and mood?

Are they healthy for you in the short and long term?

What activities or habits give you energy? Do you listen to your body's signals? Why or why not?

Is it time rest or time to get moving?

How do you speak to yourself when you are feeling unmotivated?

What would change if you replaced criticism with encouragement?

Discipline is a tuffy: what's really stopping you from finding the energy to act?

What are your daily nutrition and workout goals? How can you make them more manageable and consistent?

What motivates you to care for your body and prioritize your health?

What external forces—people, routines, or surroundings—seem to siphon your light, leaving you feeling depleted or off-center?

Which people, habits or milieu amplify your illumination by strengthening your sense of clarity and presence?

The RBC's Relationships. Bonds. Connections.

Evaluate each of your relationships: What are their gifts and drawbacks?

Do these connections honor your values, protect your boundaries, and nurture your becoming?

Do they leave you at ease, uplifted, and alive with inspiration?

Are the patterns in your connections healthy or unhealthy? If so, what might they tell about yourself, others, and the nature of your relationships?

How do you communicate during conflicts? How can you maintain peace?

Which relationships in your life inspire you and what makes them so meaningful?

What are the relationships that would benefit you from clearer boundaries, honesty, empathy, communication, space or ?

Jumpin' Out of Your Comfy Zone

Do you venture out of your standard operating mode and safety nets?

What fears hold you back from exploring the unknown and new opportunities?

What is one manageable action you can take today that gently challenges you while improving your quality of life?

Goal Brackets:

Shortie... 1 Year

Midie... 5 Years

Ladies Length... 10+ years

What are three goals you would like to accomplish? What specific actions can you take to ensure you achieve these goals?

What milestones can you set to track progress?

What challenges do you foresee, and how can you prepare to overcome them?

What does your dream life look like? Is this dream realistically attainable? Why or why not?

What resources, relationships, or skills do you need to transform this vision into reality?

Rip the Masking Tape Off Your Eyeballz:

What stories are you selling yourself?

Are your actions writing the next chapter, or are they stuck in fiction?

What are the current pros and cons in your life—across everything under the sun and the moon?

Gold Rush
Flush Wit' It

Its not how much money you rake in—it's about how much green you are stackin' for a rainy day.

How much gold are you pilin' up for the oopsy-reserve or life's *fun* surprises?

Does your lifestyle align with your income and long-term financial goals? If not, what specific adjustments can you make to live within your means while still working toward your aspirations?

How does your spending reflect your values and priorities? Are you on the right path to retiring comfortably one day?

What strategies, habits, or financial practices can you adopt to improve your future financial security?

What is one thing you can implement today to bring you closer to your financial needs, wishes and dreams?

Self-Mastery with God's Guidance

Do you help others in the same way you wish to be supported?

How can your communication improve so you do not embitter or embarrass the person you are talking to or about?

What mindful acts can you implement to be respectful and avoid judging others?

How does humility show up as awareness rather than self-erasure?

Where in your life are you being asked to lead with integrity and act in alignment with justice, clarity, and courage?

How can you cultivate a life lived blamelessly—to be free from the weight of resentment and regret?

What steps can you take to stay focused on resolving the problems in your life?

Repentance is the umpteen opportunity to realign with your soul and life's purpose. Acceptance and/or forgiveness are offerings you can make for your own peace.

When the actions of others cannot be forgiven—at least for now or perhaps never—how might acceptance become the sacred act that loosens your grip, allowing you to let go and move forward in a state of inner prosperity?

How do you practice self-discipline so that you may overcome wandering desires: gluttony, pride, greed, lust, envy, wrath, and sloth?

What are your favorite Proverbs, Psalms, and Verses?

What do they mean to you, and how have they improved your outlook on life?

PERFECTLY³

Persevere Peacefully through Passion.

Enthusiastically Explore
while Evolving Righteously
and Respectfully.

Rejoice in Faith and Forge ahead in life
through Forgiveness.

Encourage, Empower,
and Enlighten with the Confidence
and Clarity to Commit to the Truth
while embodying Thankfulness
and Thoughtfulness.

Level up while Laughing and Loving.

Yes, to Yin and Yang.

TIL' NEXT TIME!

Dear Page-Turner Enthusiasts,

A heartfelt thank you for giving my verbal flurry a chance. Pouring these chaotic reflections and broken pieces of my life onto these tree-skinz has been a wild, cathartic ride.

Now, it's time to let my cerebral casserole cool off so I can take a few extended cat naps before pouncing on my next scrumptious creation. I have a couple of recipes brewing, just need to lock down some rare ingredients.

Until then, lets connect!

I would love to hear your stories, random thoughts, and of course, any feedback you may want to throw my way...

With Gratitude,
and a Dash of Sass-i-Tude,

Monique

www.BoldChaosTheory.com

Prayer from Me...

In the darkest valleys of trials and tribulations, may you be wrapped in His unshakable protection, filled with a peace that surpasses understanding, as it grants you the divine clarity to see the right path forward in your time of need.

May your spirit remain steadfast, your heart unburdened of fear, and your steps guided with unwavering faith in yourself as you rise above every obstacle before you.

What seeks to break you shall only build you, and what feels impossible now, let it change course to uplift you through the power of His grace.

Amen.

Random Thoughts